*Also by Ivan Butler and published
by Tantivy/Barnes*

CINEMA IN BRITAIN: An Illustrated Survey
HORROR IN THE CINEMA
THE CINEMA OF ROMAN POLANSKI
RELIGION IN THE CINEMA

THE
WAR FILM

IVAN BUTLER

South Brunswick and New York: A. S. Barnes and Company
London: The Tantivy Press

© 1974 by Ivan Butler

A. S. Barnes & Co. Inc.
Cranbury
New Jersey 08512

The Tantivy Press
108 New Bond Street
London W1Y OQX

Library of Congress Cataloging in Publication Data

Butler, Ivan.
    The war film.

      "Chronological list of war films": p.
      1. War films—History and criticism. I. Title.
PN1995.9.W3B8   791.43'7   73-3765
ISBN 0-498-01395-2

Jacket design (featuring Jack Palance in ATTACK!)
by Stefan Dreja

SBN 904208 10 9 (U.K.)
Printed in the United States of America

To Falkland in friendship

Contents

Acknowledgments

I am grateful to the following for the generous loan of stills: Peter Cowie, Roger Manvell, Barrie Pattison, Tony Slide and Maurice Speed—and also to the following companies: 20th Century-Fox, United Artists, Universal-International, B.I.F., G.F.D., Paramount, British Lion, DEFA, Metro-Goldwyn-Mayer, Columbia, Warner Brothers, Miracle Films, Svensk Film-industri, Associated British-Pathe, Group Films, Rank Organisation.

My thanks are also due to Derek Elley and Charles Swynnerton for their constructive help in editing and collating the book, and to my wife for reading the proofs.

I.B.

George C. Scott playing the title role in the most successful of recent war films—PATTON

Introduction

THIS BOOK is a study of the main trends in the treatment of war by the fictional cinema. It is not intended as a sociological or political treatise—though such aspects are of course inseparable from such a theme; neither does it touch on film aesthetics, a subject with which most war films are notably—and perhaps not unmercifully—unconcerned.

I have confined myself to films shown in Britain and America, and largely to those made in the two countries. Documentaries are touched on only briefly. Even within these limitations the subject is so vast that it has proved necessary to be somewhat selective. Merely to list the titles of all films concerned with war and its effects would probably fill a book of this length. The term "war film" I have defined as concerned either directly with the actual fighting, or very closely with the effects and aftermath of a conflict. "Fringe films" such as the Cold War spy cycles or those of prewar Nazi Germany have in general been omitted. Being selective, of course, means being subjective, and omissions may be dictated by unconscious as well as conscious choice. I hope, however, that few if any "important" productions have been forgotten.

Though I do not claim to have seen every film mentioned, at least during the earlier years, I am sufficiently advanced on my journey towards the final fade-out to be able to remember the impact of silent movies from the end of the First World War at the time they were first shown—even if some of the details have faded. I can recall the squishing of tear-sodden handkerchiefs all round me at the early screening of *The Four Horsemen of the Apocalypse* (1921), as Alice Terry tended her blinded husband accompanied by a soulful soprano standing by the side of the screen and singing (with Valentino in mind, of course) "I think of all you are to me—I think of all you cannot be . . ." It is a scene that would probably pipe few eyes today— a fact, I would emphasise, that cannot *in itself* be held against such a film made for its own time.

The record of the cinema in or about war is not a particularly edifying one. Pusillanimity has in general been the order of the day. With fawning eagerness the war film has offered itself as a medium of propaganda (the supreme one), and the money to be made by toeing the line appears to have been an ever-present and overriding consideration. Rarely, if ever, has it gone against the trend.

When *All Quiet on the Western Front* (1930) first came out it was hailed in some quarters as a "courageous" production. This is nonsense. It was a pacifist film launched (very profitably) during a pacifist period. To be "courageous," it (or something similar—the book was not in existence until the late Twenties) should have been made in the middle of the war. Admittedly film-making is an expensive business; admittedly films can be suppressed by governments, religious bodies, military influence; but both the graphic and the literary "arts" retained here and there some small degree of independent thought. If one of the prerequisites of Art is that it knows no frontiers (which does not mean merely the physical boundaries of the world's countries), then the cinema—in the sphere of war at any rate—must gracefully renounce its claims.

A major decision to be made in setting out this book was whether to group the films according to the particular war they dealt with or relate them to the period in which they were made. I eventually decided on the latter, feeling that the interest of a production such as *Paths of Glory* is as a film of 1958 rather than of the First World War. However, to balance this the index has been arranged sectionally by wars. It is probable that anyone anxious to look up, say, *Oh! What a Lovely War* (1969), already knows to which section he should turn.

Chapter divisions are, of course, to some extent arbitrary: not every film made in the mid-Twenties was nostalgic, nor did every production of the early Thirties regard war with a disillusioned eye.

1. Primitives.
As the Clouds Gather

IN 1897, only a few hours after the United States declared war on Spain, Albert Smith and the British-born J. Stuart Blackton produced for the Vitagraph Company *Tearing Down the Spanish Flag*. This brief patriotic super-film—made during one night in a room at the top of the Morse Building—may well have been the first commercial war picture to have been made. It was extremely successful and set the tone for a type of militant propaganda to be followed and developed for years to come.

In subsequent pre-First World War films the American studios poured forth a constant and popular stream of films dramatising the honour and glory of Army and Navy—at work in the Philippines, in South America, during the American Revolution and the Civil War. With titles such as *A Day with the Soldier Boys, Rally round the Flag, Faithful unto Death* (1913), and *None but the Brave Deserve the Fair,* they were in effect recruiting posters that moved, calculated to stir the emotions and stun the intelligence. Edison used the Spanish war as background for his *Romance of a War Nurse* (1908). Norma Talmadge made an early appearance in a one-reeler, *The Dixie Mother* (1910), which starred Florence Turner as a formidably patriotic matriarch who despatched no fewer than six sons to the American Civil War, and went mad (a little tardily, perhaps) when the youngest was killed. One of D. W. Griffith's early attempts to use a large canvas was *The Battle* (1911), a girl-and-boy story set against a Civil War background, featuring Blanche Sweet and Charles West; and in 1913 appeared the elaborate *Battle of Gettysburg* from, of all people, Mack Sennett.

In Britain it is interesting to compare the pre-Boer War film *The Deserter* (1898, R. W. Paul) with Cecil Hepworth's *The Call to Arms* of 1902: the former treated the escape and re-arrest of an army deserter with sympathy; the latter, made while the war was still dragging

13

on, depicted a "lounge lizard" who becomes imbued with the martial spirit and turns into a brave fighting man. During the war Paul himself made a series of propaganda shorts on army life.

The see-what-will-happen-if-you-don't-watch-out school of drama sprang to life first in the theatre, with the production in 1909 of the famous admonitory play *An Englishman's Home*. The author, proudly if a little smugly designating himself "A Patriot," was Sir Guy du Maurier, and the play showed the dire results of "unpreparedness" when a country house is invaded by foreign soldiery who burst in through the who's-for-tennis french windows intent on espionage, glass-cabinet smashing, and rape. The play was to be made into a film of unbelievable *naïveté* towards the end of the Thirties. Also in 1909, Charles Urban's *The Airship Destroyer* foretold an aerial bombardment foiled by the use of a flying torpedo. The inventor was inspired not by love of country but by seeing a bomb land on his girl-friend's roof, a less exalted but more readily understandable reason. Only a few months before the First World War broke out, Harold Shaw produced *England's Menace* (1914), dealing with an imaginary enemy invasion of the white cliffs.

An early example of troop hiring for battle scenes occurred in Charles Weston's *The Battle of Waterloo* (1913), which featured, among other assets, a squadron of lancers.

A panoramic scene from THE BIRTH OF A NATION.

14

Germany produced a number of unimportant "recruitment" films, but its industry was still very much in the embryonic stage. Nor did much in the same line come from France, a country mostly engaged in faking newsreels of the Russo-Japanese war. Messrs. Bardèche and Brasillach, in their book "History of the Film," quote the astonishment of an audience presented with the spectacle of Japanese and Russian soldiers fighting to the death in front of the Chantilly grandstand. Yet nearly seventy years later, it seems, film and television viewers still believe everything they see on screens.

Italy built up a reputation for colossal and mentally stupefying spectaculars, in which the battle scenes managed to sustain audiences' attention. *The Fall of Rome* (1913/14), *The Napoleonic Epic* (1913) and *Julius Caesar* (1913/14) were among the titles, but the most famous was *Cabiria* (1914), directed by Piero Fosco (from a scenario by Gabriele d'Annunzio). Visually and technically this epic of the Punic Wars was impressive. Taking two years to make (1912–14) and costing $250,000, it featured sieges, vast *mêlées* and the crossing of the Alps. An added attraction was the star, Maciste, according to legend a furniture remover (and thus aptly described as "the gentle giant"), who "picked up women as if they were feathers." With all this, and Hannibal too, war was indeed a "glorious adventure."

The most memorable film of the period was Griffith's *The Birth of a Nation,* which, though not generally shown until 1915, was conceived in the spring of the previous year. Griffith based his story on two novels by the Reverend Thomas Dixon, "The Clansman" and "The Leopard's Spots," though according to Lillian Gish he had no need of either except as a basis of confidence for so large an undertaking. The sweep and vigour of the battle scenes have rarely been surpassed. Famous sequences such as the March to the Sea—opening from a tiny iris in a corner of the screen showing a weeping woman and her children by their ruined home, and widening to a vast panorama of armies, wagons and burning buildings—can still astonish after nearly sixty years. Equally effective are the quieter moments, such as the famous shot of the mother's hand drawing her returning soldier son through the doorway of their home. Tremendous in scope though the war scenes are, however, *The Birth of a Nation* is not primarily a war film—nations are not born by tearing themselves apart. Griffith depicts all the suffering brought about by disaster, but it is with a compassion unfired by anger. More to his purpose, it seems, is that we should share the terror of Lillian Gish imprisoned with her would-be ravisher. The core of Griffith's masterpiece is the Reconstruction of the South sequence, and here the agonising aftermath of war—seen

Robert Harron in fighting mood.

from the viewpoint of the defeated Southerner—is shown with a power only rarely equalled since.

In the period between the conception and delivery of this peak film the First World War began, and the cinema—American and European alike—started on the downward track, almost deliberately it seemed, towards one of its regrettably frequent nadirs.

2. The First World War

THE OUTBREAK OF THE WAR in Europe in 1914 found the cinema of the United States in a pacifist mood, rather strangely at variance with its rally-round-the-flag-boys trumpetings of a few years previously. This was in line with the President's "Keep Out" policy, and titles such as *Be Neutral, Neutrality, War Is Hell* (1914) and *The Horrors of War* (1914) are indicative of the general trend. *The White Sister*, made by Essanay in 1915 and starring Viola Allan, was based on a novel about a young Italian girl who enters a nunnery when she hears her soldier lover has been killed. It took a definite anti-war stand from the viewpoint of Christian objection, and was re-made first in 1922 with Henry King directing Ronald Colman and Lillian Gish (in one of her most beautiful performances), and again in 1933 (Helen Hayes and Clark Gable directed by Victor Fleming), both periods of pacifism.

Films were to some extent imported from Germany (*The German Side of the War, The Cruise of the M*) and Britain (*The Battling British, The Great European War,* 1914; *England's Menace*) to preserve an even balance.

The most distinguished and sincere film of the period was Herbert Brenon's *War Brides* (1916), in which Alla Nazimova plays a young wife, Joan, who, when her husband is killed in a war, refuses to obey a royal decree that all available single women should marry and bear children to carry on the fighting. At the climax of the film the head of the country tells her that wars are inevitable, whereupon Joan, who is expecting the child of her dead husband, cries "No more children for war," and kills herself. This semi-Lysistratan theme is put over with considerable power, and it is a pity that the existing stills show absurdly over-dramatic poses because Nazimova, who suffers particularly in this respect, in fact gives a performance of tragic integrity. Though the country at war is unspecified, the brutal soldiery have a distinctly Teutonic appearance. *War Brides* was suppressed when the nation that championed free speech entered the war.

Much more dubious in intention was the other major supposedly

Battle carnage from Thomas Ince's CIVILIZATION.

pacifist production of the early war years, *Civilization* (1916), directed by the Janus-faced Thomas Ince who had previously made *The Coward* (1915, about a brave pacifist who went into uniform after all), and who was afterwards to go hell-for-leather into pro-war production. *Civilization,* a competently made but nauseatingly dishonest film, tells of a submarine engineer whose body is taken over by the spirit of Christ and used as a mouthpiece against "war." Though reputed to have helped Wilson's re-election on his "Keep Out" platform, it is cunningly calculated to direct an audience's hatred towards a specific enemy rather than against the notion of war itself: not cunningly enough, however, to fool the Swedes, who considered that the "enemy" so closely resembled the Germans as to make the film unsuitable for showing in a truly neutral country.

As early as 1915 (a year before *War Brides*) the tide began to turn, when J. Stuart Blackton (producer of *Tearing Down the Spanish Flag*) brought out a work with the unpleasantly ambiguous title *The Battle Cry of Peace.* The plot was taken from a story by Hudson Maxim (of machine-gun fame) called "Defenceless America," and was a strident shriek for more armaments as the only means of protecting the nation's womanhood from the Huns—who were portrayed, as from

18

now, as leering, lusting, licentious and ludicrously caricatured monsters. No less a personage than Theodore Roosevelt was interested in this production—which made it not a whit less lamentable. Henry Ford inserted large announcements in the press pointing out that the whole thing was nothing less than a profit-producing stunt for Maxim's business. The film, however, which starred Norma Talmadge and Charles Richman, had the desired inflammatory effect and opened the gates to a flood of melodramas differing only in degrees of absurdity. Pacifists saw the error of their ways; those who adhered to their convictions were morons or traitors; stainless womanhood was heavily besmirched by oafish Prussian subhumans (the anonymity of earlier films was soon unveiled); and dunderheaded German spies were effortlessly unmasked. The abysmal stupidity of the enemy was to be played up in the Second World War also, it being overlooked apparently that the duller the foe the less credit there is in beating him, and the more reprehensible the time it takes to do so.

Brenon's sincere and moving *War Brides* was travestied in a William Fox production, *The War Bride's Secret* (1916, Kenean Buel) one of the earlier pictures to make capital (literally) from alleged "atrocities." A famous serial backed by William Randolph Hearst and entitled *Patria* (1916) turned on the Japanese and propagandised against them for a change. Unfortunately Japan was friendly towards Britain at that time, so in the middle of events their nationality had to be changed—an embarrassing situation that was to plague over-eager film-makers again in later years.

Among this sorry group *The Fall of a Nation* stands out in its silliness (a silliness apparent even in the extant stills)—crudely caricaturing William Jennings Bryan and others (including the clergy) for their beliefs. It was written and produced by the Reverend Thomas Dixon, and once again a mythical enemy looked strangely like the Germans.

Cecil B. DeMille came along to turn history inside out in order to use Joan of Arc as contemporary propaganda. *Joan the Woman* (1917) is first enveloped in a ridiculous modern wrapping, in which a soldier, Eric Trent, is inspired to go on a fatal mission by a vision of Joan after he has found an old sword supposed to have belonged to her. The story then reverts to Joan herself, who is engaged in a highly improbable love affair with an English soldier—Eric Trent himself, who later betrays her to the Burgundians! This treachery inevitably means that Britain (and America) are morally bound to go to the aid of France in 1914 in order to expiate the crime of the terrible, if long-dead, Eric. Wallace Reid and Geraldine Farrar, plus

THE LITTLE AMERICAN: Mary Pickford in danger.

copious spectacle, helped to carry audiences through this farrago; and DeMille, after a brief rest with *Romance of the Redwoods* (1917), returned to the fray with *The Little American* (1917).

This picture, perhaps the most famous of its kind, was released just after America entered the war. In it Mary Pickford, the World's Sweetheart, undergoes every conceivable kind of indignity at the hands of the enemy: nearly drowned in a torpedoed liner (but saved in time), nearly raped in the dark by a former sweetheart (but saved in time—the light came on), nearly shot as a spy (but saved in time). This was cunning casting—an insult that called for the uttermost retribution. The moral implications of *The Little American,* however, are dubious in the extreme. For instance, the German-American semi-hero (played by Jack Holt), who once loved Mary and is later called to the Kaiser's colours, is favourably regarded for betraying his country (and saving Mary), but no fate is too bad for betrayal in the opposite direction. There is also some sickening "symbolism" involving a shattered Calvary, and the usual caricatured villains, with Walter Long and Wallace Beery obviously enjoying themselves hugely as libidinous Huns. Technically much of the production was, for its time, outstanding. The sinking of the "Lusitania" (thinly disguised as the "Vertania") with the terrified diners, the gay table trimmings floating higher and higher up the saloon walls, and Mary in her party dress in water up to her pretty waist, remains vividly in the memory over the years. It was, however, a blatantly opportunist production —as DeMille disarmingly remarks, *"The Little American* was timely, as I had known months before it would be."

With war finally declared, all restraint could be cast aside. In 1916 Griffith had brought out his great *Intolerance*—an ironic title for the times. Later he was invited to photograph the war at the Front, and was himself proudly photographed in full uniform. Part of the result of the trip was *Hearts of the World* (1918), dealing with the plight of a French village under German occupation. Griffith's sentimentality is given full rein in so promising a field. However, though once more portraying the enemy as monsters of infamy, and glorying in such captions as "Month after month piled up with its legend of Hunnish crimes on the book of God," the film contained, on the credit side, some reasonably realistic frontline scenes, and sensitive performances

Lillian Gish traversing the battlefield in HEARTS OF THE WORLD.

from Lillian Gish and Robert Harron—with Noël Coward making his screen *début* in a tiny part. The scene where the distraught girl wanders around the battlefield trailing her wedding-dress remains classic, if improbable.

Cecil B. DeMille returned in form with another war epic (released 1918) entitled *Till I Come Back to You,* about a Belgian girl, married before the war to a German who afterwards admits he is a spy and enlists in the German army. A Captain Jefferson Strong (with such a name, naturally, a hero) pretends to be the German in order to destroy certain terror weapons. As he is about to blow up the installation, however, he comes across the Belgian girl in charge of a number of war orphans. To avoid killing them also he disobeys orders, and at the court martial that follows he is pardoned by King Albert of the Belgians himself. The German dies, Strong marries the widow, and audiences presumably went home satisfied. The villain is played by a fine character actor, G. Butler Clonbough, *alias* (in peace time) Gustav von Seyffertitz.

The sinking of the "Lusitania" was a godsend to other producers besides DeMille, and it was also the subject of the first feature-length cartoon by Winsor McCay, of *Gertie the Dinosaur* fame.

The death of Nurse Edith Cavell was another bonanza for atrocity hunters and featured directly or indirectly in several films. There were also *The Hun Within* (1918), *War and the Woman, The Kaiser—Beast of Berlin* (there was to be a *Hitler—Beast of Berlin,* 1948, in due course), *For Valor, Shame* (far from Bergman), *To Hell with the Kaiser, A Little Patriot* (child-star Baby Peggy, after a vision of herself as Joan of Arc, encouraging fellow babies to expectorate on slacking daddies), *Lest We Forget, The Man Who Was Afraid, The Evil Eye* (Kaiser Wilhelm's, naturally), and so on *ad nauseam. The Unpardonable Sin* (directed by Marshall Neilan), in which Blanche Sweet rescues a sister in Belgium and suffers the usual treatment from Wallace Beery, was unhappily held up by production problems until 1919, when it was to late for it to be enjoyed in the proper spirit.

In his book on "Hollywood—The Golden Era" Jack Spears expresses his opinion that except for the classic Chaplin comedies Hollywood failed to produce a single noteworthy motion picture during the barren war years. This is harsh judgement, but difficult to counter. Certainly, if all the film cans were collected together in a building that caught fire, Chaplin's *Shoulder Arms* (1918) would be the first to be rescued. Despite the comic exaggeration, its picture of the misery and physical discomfort of trench life is probably the closest to reality. The film was released to a war-weary world only a few weeks before

Charlie Chaplin in SHOULDER ARMS: Sydney Chaplin on the right.

the Armistice and amid some trepidation as to how it would be received. The worry was needless.

The most ironic comedy of the war years in the American cinema, however, was one that actually took place. A producer named Robert Goldstein made a film called *The Spirit of '76* (1917), about the Americans throwing off the British yoke. Unfortunately, it was released about the time that the Americans joined the British to throw off the threat of a German yoke. The film was alleged to have been made by enemy aliens, and Goldstein went to prison for ten years.

*　　*　　*

Though Britain produced a large number of "war dramas" they were, understandably, a good deal less ambitious than those from America. Perhaps because the war was more of a stark reality they were also, on the whole, much less hysterically bellicose, much less full of atrocities and caricature.

The Great European War (1914), rushed into its planning stage during a session at Frascati's Restaurant the very day war broke out, was a form of fictionalised newsreel documentary compiled by George Pearson and G. B. Samuelson. Employing every actor available at

23

short notice to represent the Kaiser, Sir Edward Grey, Kitchener, the Tsar, etc., it followed the course of events that led to the start of hostilities. It was frankly dramatised fact, clear of the dubious methods employed later in other faked-fact battle films, and was shown in America, doubtless to encourage the people to participate.

Typical of the first years were such productions as *The German Spy Peril* (1914, Barker Company), in which a young man overhears some singularly tactless German spies planning to blow up the Houses of Parliament and after various adventures manages to blow up the spies instead: he thereupon receives the gratitude of his King and country, who are rather touchingly confident that, with the politicians safe, all will be well. Others were *Christmas without Daddy* (1914, British and Colonial, generally known as B. and C.); *1914* (1915, London Film Company); *Unfit* or *The Strength of the Weak* (1915, Cecil Hepworth) about a young man who is turned down by the Forces but "does his bit" at home); *His Country's Bidding* (1914, Cecil Hepworth); *Saving the Colours* (1914, B. and C.). This last concerns a wife who shames her reluctant husband by enlisting as a nurse and then—by a wonderful chance—nurses him back to life after, duly shamed, he has joined up and fetched himself a "Blighty."

As the war dragged on, however, such patriotic pieces lost their appeal and, with plenty to escape from, escapism became the order of the day. Hepworth ingeniously managed to combine escapism and realism in *The Outrage* (1915), a story, written by Albert Chevalier, that took place during the age of chivalry but managed to reflect the alleged German atrocities of 1914. Henry Ainley and Alma Taylor starred.

The first of a famous series of "battle" films appeared in 1916—*The Battle of the Somme*, by Geoffrey Malins and J. B. McDowell. It is documentation rather than reportage, proved immensely popular, and was followed in due course by *Arras, Ancre* and *St. Quentin*, all from the same firm in 1917.

Towards the end of the period two films appeared from Welsh-Pearson (Thomas Welsh and George Pearson) that should be mentioned. *The Better 'Ole* (1918) is a mild comedy based on the famous Bruce Bairnsfather cartoon characters. It opens with a shot of the three musketeers singing "One for all . . .", moves to the present day, and closes with the three Tommies going over the top. Its message, Pearson said, was "Carry On—and nothing more." Another version was made in America by Warner Brothers in 1926, directed by Charles Reisner, with Syd Chaplin as Old Bill. It contained a number of well-staged "serious" war scenes, but the mountainous surroundings

THE BETTER 'OLE: Charles Rock, Hugh E. Wright, Arthur Cleave.

Gallant childhood: **THE GREAT EUROPEAN WAR.**

George Pearson's KIDDIES IN THE RUINS.

must have surprised the inhabitants of Northern France.

The second Welsh-Pearson production, issued the same year, was *Kiddies in the Ruins,* an odd little three-reeler of children at play in the ruins of their French town. Filmed in a Paris suburb, it could have developed as a precursor of the Italian neo-realist school years later, but settled instead for a straight story of comedy and thrills.

Another oddity was Herbert Brenon's *Invasion of Britain* (1918), intended as a major spectacle but too long in the making and eventually shelved. A part of it, after a brief trench scene, concentrates on a woman in her cottage hearing first that her eldest son has been killed as her youngest departs for the front, and then that her grandson is lost in an air-raid. Ellen Terry and José Collins appeared in this tale of a much-troubled mother. In the same year a Hepworth production, *Broken in the Wars,* dealt with government aid for discharged fighting men. The Minister of Pensions explains to Joe, a wounded shoemaker, how he will be helped to start up again in his own business. Joe prospers, the Ministry builds itself a good image, and everyone is happy—except perhaps those able to foresee the slump-darkened future.

A left-over that came out in 1919 was the first production of the Stoll Company, entitled *Comradeship,* directed by Maurice Elvey. Starring Gerald Ames, it told a moderately tall story of a pacifist who sees the light, goes to the front, saves the life of a friend who, he thinks, is the one his own girl really loves, and is blinded. In a blissful ending, however, he recovers both girl and sight. Self-sacrifice in a war film not only pays, but must be seen to pay.

* * *

As was to be expected, few films from foreign countries reached English-speaking audiences. Mention should perhaps be made of Abel Gance's *J'accuse* (1919), a sometimes impressive but generally confused melodrama in which a soldier, driven mad after a German had raped his wife and left her with child (the soldier thinks his best friend is responsible), claims that he is called "J'accuse," and commands the dead to rise and fight again. This they duly do—led by the Gaul chieftain Vercingetorix. The film was made with the help of the Army Cinematograph Service but Gance himself was accused of having injected it with the poison of pacifism. A few years later (1925) he produced his vast triple-screen essay in hero-worship of the arch-militarist Napoléon.

J'ACCUSE: Abel Gance's silent film.

Two scenes from REVEILLE: Betty Balfour, and (below) with Ralph Forbes.

3. Period of Nostalgia

THE GREATER PROPORTION of British and American films during the First World War were basically boy-and-girl stories, flavoured with varying amounts of propaganda and set against the convenient, profitable and photogenic background of the conflict. With the cessation of hostilities, however, the interest of audiences rapidly dwindled. Apart from a few unimportant latecomers caught by the Armistice, the recent war vanished almost completely from the screen, and fictional characters worked out their personal relationships against the less violent backcloths of older struggles, such as that between Cavalier and Roundhead (*The Breed of the Treshams,* 1920, starring Martin Harvey and directed by Kenelm Foss; *Royal Oak,* 1924, with Henry Ainley, Clive Brook and Betty Compson, directed by Maurice Elvey), or between North and South (the story sequence from Harold Lloyd's *Grandma's Boy,* 1922).

Documentary included the well-made *Battle of Jutland* (1921) from British Instructional Films—their first production—making use of animated models, newsreels, maps and studio reconstructions to re-create the great sea battle.

Germany, Britain and America, however, each produced one important film concerned with the First World War during the lull before King Vidor's *The Big Parade* (1925). From Britain came *Reveille* (1924), one of George Pearson's most successful productions. Gentle, slow, low-keyed, constructed in accordance with his theory that in treating subjects of high significance theme is more important than plot, it tells an episodic story of ordinary people and their suffering as a result of the war. There is a famous moment depicting the Two Minutes Silence, where for the entire duration the director renounces all movement except the gentle brushing of a lace curtain against a woman's face as she looks out of a window. At the first presentation the orchestra fell silent to match the stillness on the screen. Effects of this kind—nowadays either *clichés* or gimmicks—were in those days courageously unconventional.

29

G. W. Pabst's *The Joyless Street (Die freudlose Gasse)*, from Germany in 1925, is a grim picture of war's dreary aftermath in a defeated country. Set in Vienna, it compares interestingly with Carol Reed's depiction of a similar period in the same town after the Second World War, *The Third Man* (1949). The film is noted now mainly for the appearance of the young Greta Garbo, but it is a powerful and uncompromising work. Pabst is said to have been influenced to some extent by D. W. Griffith, who in 1924 went to Germany and came back with *It's a Wonderful Life,* a slow, drab, sometimes sentimental but often extremely moving film of hardship and love in a shattered countryside. Though no masterpiece, it is one of Griffith's most underrated films, telling its story of a Polish family trying to settle in Germany with a deep compassion and a warm plea for tolerance and forgiveness.

The interest of the third film referred to, Rex Ingram's *The Four Horsemen of the Apocalypse* (1921), lies less in its intrinsic merits or demerits than in its position in time. It is, in fact, a key production in any survey of the subject. The intention of the makers seems to have been to produce an anti-war film—wild coincidences are contrived to point the tragic irony of former friends meeting on opposing sides and being blown up together, and the grief and waste are emphasised. Against these worthy sentiments, however, are ranged all the *clichés* of the pro-war patriotic saga: villainous monster-Huns or moronic wooden-headed ones, a former pacifist (Josef Swickard) who is brought to view his beliefs with shame, a handsome feckless young man who is "regenerated" and meets death on the field of glory, the exhilarating movement and destruction of battle. So vile was the behaviour of the licentious soldiery when it took possession of the *château* (even to dancing down the stairs in women's underclothing) that a whole sequence was cut from later versions in order not to upset the now-forgiven Germans, and replaced by a tame and tantalising title saying "After a night of shame and terror," or words to that effect. Yet this whole film was made and shown after the shame and terror were over: in a sense, though no poem, it is emotion recollected in tranquillity—and surely with a touch of embarrassment. Nevertheless, quite apart from Valentino, its effect at the time was overwhelming. Without any doubt it exactly caught the mood of the moment, bridging the gap between exhausted satiety and nostalgia, and also affording a last enjoyable indulgence in Hun-phobia. The apocalyptic visions, that seem somewhat crude and flat when seen at revivals accompanied by a single piano, were tremendously impressive fifty years ago with a full-size orchestra thundering doom. At such

30

THE FOUR HORSEMEN OF THE APOCALYPSE: *Above—A Hunnish orgy; below—The enemy take over the village.*

American soldier—French village girl: John Gilbert and Renee Adoree in
THE BIG PARADE.

revivals, too, I have heard the final scene—with the mysterious Christ
figure (played by the irreplaceable Nigel de Brulier) standing with
eyes raised among the vast fields of graves and intoning "I knew them
all"—evoke jeering laughter. At the time it was as genuinely moving
as the closing sequence of *Oh! What a Lovely War*. If every other
silent war film was lost (a not too intolerable thought) *The Four
Horsemen of the Apocalypse* would preserve the atmosphere of its
period.

In addition, it made the names and fortunes of several people
connected with it, brought in a mint of money, and set its producing

company, Metro, on its way to the top of the ladder—with all that was to follow as a result.

An American picture of 1924 that is unlikely ever to achieve such glory, and which appears in only a tenth of the history books, is *The Enchanted Cottage*—in its way, an equally interesting film. It deals with the rehabilitation of a crippled and embittered war veteran when he meets a plain, lonely schoolteacher and they become beautiful in each other's eyes. Based on a play by A. W. Pinero, sensitively directed by John S. Robertson and exquisitely played by Richard Barthelmess and May McAvoy, this tender, compassionate, totally unsentimental film, despite its essentially tragic theme, was like a healing hand laid on the scars of war.

Then—in 1925—came *The Big Parade* (directed by King Vidor), the enormous success of which opened the screen to numerous films of what might be called the nostalgic period. For the rest of the silent years, with few exceptions, war was to be romanticised and glamour-ised—with some unpleasant moments of grim reality, to be sure, but mainly a matter of rowdy comradeship, pretty-French-girl-flirtations, and excitingly dramatic action. Though apparently it did not start out as one, *The Big Parade* ended up as a huge spectacular, with magnificently conceived set-pieces of advancing convoys, of a slow trek through machine-gun infested woods (timed to a metronome), of troops hurriedly evacuating a French village. The most interesting part of the film, however, is the opening sequence showing ordinary, normally intelligent men and women turned by deliberately engi-neered hysteria, aided by bands and flags, into mindless automata, fooled into participating in something they know little or nothing about—being, in fact, in Paul Rotha's expressive phrase, "howled into war."

Despite this opening, and a brief, grim shot of a line of gassed and blinded soldiers, this is in no sense an anti-war film, but rather a melodramatic boy-meets/loses/finds-girl story set against massive battle sequences. The latter, incidentally, were criticised in some con-temporary quarters for their inaccuracy. Vidor frankly confessed that moments such as the famous scene where Renée Adorée runs after John Gilbert as he leaves for the front and is left clutching his boot, were put in deliberately to "jerk a tear," and the overall impression left by the film as a whole is that a World War is awful but at least affords opportunities for teaching captivating French village girls to chew gum.

Closely following the American *Big Parade* came the British *Ma-demoiselle from Armentières* (Maurice Elvey's first Gaumont produc-

33

Estelle Brodie as MADEMOISELLE FROM ARMENTIÈRES.

tion), similar in spirit though far less ambitious in design. A straight-forward thriller, in which a French girl helps nice Englishmen to escape from the clutches of nasty Germans, it was immensely successful, cheerfully unrealistic, and made Estelle Brodie seem as much worth going to war for if you were British, as Renée Adorée was if you came from the United States.

A few other products of the nostalgic period may be mentioned. *What Price Glory?* (U.S., 1926, Raoul Walsh) softened the Stallings/Anderson anti-war play down to a knockabout comedy between two tough Marines, Captain Flagg (Victor McLaglen) and Sergeant Quirt (Edmund Lowe) squabbling over Dolores del Rio—and who wouldn't? Neither the reasonably realistic battle scenes of the Belleau Wood attack nor the classic "Stop-the-blood" outcry (contemptuously dismissed by one contemporary critic as the "sickly and obvious tragedy of the Mother's Boy") are allowed to overweigh the slapstick. So popular was this film that a sequel, *The Cock-Eyed World,* was made

34

British soldier—French village girl: Estelle Brodie and John Stuart in
MADEMOISELLE FROM ARMENTIÈRES (compare still on page 32)
Dolores del Rio prays amidst the desolation of war, in WHAT PRICE
GLORY.

in 1929, also by Raoul Walsh. This time the bone of contention—if one may so put it without disrespect—was Lili Damita.

What Price Glory? was remade in 1952 by none other than John Ford. At a time when the general level was low even for the war film it stood out surprisingly well against the trend. James Cagney and Dan Dailey were pale reflections of McLaglen and Lowe, and there is some appalling music by Jay Livingston and Ray Evans which one would imagine was inserted against the director's will, but Ford's personality gleams through occasionally, and the film's anti-war statement is brave in the vicious climate of the times.

Roses of Picardy (Britain, 1926, Maurice Elvey) took a more serious approach. A much curtailed and dramatised version of R. H. Mottram's trilogy "The Spanish Farm," it inevitably missed most of the noble sweep and breadth of that long, fine book, but is a film of much merit, very poorly served by the change of title to a hackneyed song.

Blighty (1927, Adrian Brunel) and *Poppies of Flanders* (1928, Arthur Maude) are conventional stories with a wartime setting. *Blighty,* the better of the two, was Brunel's first film for the Gainsborough company. It catches the nostalgic mood of films like *Mademoiselle from Armentières,* but unwisely tries to inject a little reality into the proceedings by cutting in shots of actual fighting. The result is merely to emphasise the unreality of the rest. *Poppies of Flanders* is from a story by Sapper and contains, according to a review of the day, "all the qualities that make for a popular success—love, laughter, patriotism and self-sacrifice." At least one is warned what to expect.

The Guns of Loos (1928, Sinclair Hill) manages to achieve a slightly new angle, combining a picture of the home with that of the trenches. The owner of a steel works converted to a munitions factory (Henry Victor) goes to France, is accused of cowardice—in reality suffering from shell-shock—redeems himself by saving the guns, and becoming blinded in the process, returns home in time to dissuade his munition workers from going on strike. Though the sentiments were monotonously impeccable, the director manages to keep events moving, particularly during the well-staged war scenes. These, when the film opened at the Plaza Cinema in London, were shown through an enlarging device known as the "Magnascope."

Magnascoped or not, a far more worthwhile film was Herbert Wilcox's *Dawn* (1928), about Nurse Edith Cavell. The tragedy of her execution had been blatantly distorted into anti-Hun propaganda in several cheap wartime pictures; here it is told with grief but without bias or rancour—a tragedy perhaps, but not an atrocity. Nurse Cavell

36

Godfrey Winn meets Jameson Thomas in BLIGHTY.

knew perfectly well that if she were caught the penalty for helping
members of the Allies over the frontier would be death: the Germans
shot her, unwillingly but inevitably, as a deterrent, and as a punish-
ment for the breaking of martial law. Wilcox records rather than
comments, allowing the events to speak for themselves, and his film
is irradiated by Sybil Thorndike's fine and warmly human performance. Release of the film was held up through groundless fears that
the ex-enemy might be offended: the resultant publicity was, it is to
be hoped, of benefit to all concerned. Wilcox was to retell the story
with no less integrity and compassion in 1939, drawing from Anna
Neagle her best performance.

Of much more massive scope than any of these British productions
was the American spectacular *Wings* (1927, William Wellman), the

first of the large-scale air epics that left a not-wholly-welcome legacy lasting to the present day. Even now the innovatory scenes of aerial combat can catch the breath. The film was originally shown—in London, at any rate—on an expanding screen in much the same way as *The Guns of Loos,* and the first occasion on which the small rectangle suddenly and unexpectedly burst its bounds into a huge panorama of sky and planes was as thrilling as the preview of Cinerama. Unfortunately, apart from the flying sequences, and a momentary appearance of Gary Cooper as a doomed aviator, *Wings* is almost totally devoid of interest—a trite triangle story that seems to entangle itself interminably, plus a few pious war-is-hell platitudes. There is, however, always Clara Bow, looking bewitching in Red Cross uniform.

Close on the heels of *Wings,* as it were, followed *Lilac Time* (George Fitzmaurice), *Captain Swagger* (Edward H. Griffith) and *Legion of the Condemned* (William Wellman), all in 1928. The first, loosely adapted from a Broadway play of several years earlier, featured

A spectacular battle scene from William Wellman's WINGS.

Colleen Moore as a French girl and Gary Cooper as a British airman. It has some effective aerial sequences but is mostly background romance. Born on the edge of the sound era, it was released with added effects: a theme song, "Jeannine, I Dream of Lilac Time," just about sums it up. *Captain Swagger*, with Rod la Rocque as an American in the French Air Force, and Sue Carol as compensation, is equal hokum, but is done with a certain sparkle in both direction and playing. *The Legion of the Condemned* was Wellman's attempt to follow *Wings*, but after a promising start, gathering together a number of men who, at the outbreak of war, migrate to the Flying Squadron of the Foreign Legion, the Lafayette Escadrille, the film bogs down in the usual fictional quagmire. Gary Cooper, apparently condemned at this period to fatal aviation, joins the group. With features all a-twist, he tells a prostitute (undefined as such, naturally, in those days) the tale of his betrayal by a woman. As a young reporter, he says, he had been sent to cover an Embassy ball, taking with him his girl-friend. After a few dances he lost her, only to find her again later in a private room, a state of intoxication, and the arms of a licentious Baron. To cap all, he heard her say (by subtitle): "He is only a young fool I have been amusing myself with." Understandably, he finished off his unsuccessful evening by rushing out to join the Foreign Legion. As he recounts this frightful drama of female perfidy to the sympathetic tart he slowly tears a white carnation to pieces and allows the petals to flutter to the ground. Later, he is sent on a special mission to lead a lady spy behind the enemy lines. She arrives, all muffled up—but it is no surprise, except to him, when her identity is revealed. She is, naturally, caught by the enemy and put before a firing squad, but rescued, naturally, by our hero. Though a little extreme, this type of picture is fairly typical of the average war film of the time. No amount of skyrobatics can save it.

Things were a little better on the factual side. Britain producing such reconstructions as *Armageddon* (1923), *Zeebrugge* (1924), *Ypres* (1925), *Mons* (1926) and *The Battle of the Coronel and Falkland Islands* (1927), all from BIF; and *The Somme* (1927) and *Q Ships* (1928) from New Era. Though not without their critics they were in general received with respect if not enthusiasm. *Armageddon* (following Allenby's campaign in Palestine) and *Zeebrugge* were directed by H. Bruce Woolfe; *Ypres*, *Mons*, and *Coronel and Falkland* (most successful of all) by Walter Summers; *The Somme* by M. A. Wetherell; *Q Ships* by Geoffrey Barkas and Michael Barringer.

From France, in the same style, came Léon Poirier's *Verdun* (1927); from Germany *The Emden* (1927, the Emelka Company of

Munich). The full title of the former is *Verdun, visions d'histoire:* more dramatised than the British series, it is an odd mixture of bombast and deep sincerity, undeniably impressive despite moments of inflated symbolism. The German film is a dignified account of the famous cruiser, somewhat marred by fictional embellishments.

* * *

With so much recent material to hand, it was hardly surprising that more distant wars received scant attention during the period. The American Civil War was given its fullest treatment in *The General* (1926) Buster Keaton's best-known (though not, perhaps, his best) comedy. The story of the locomotive stolen by the Yankees and rescued by its Confederate driver is founded on a true incident, and exceptional care has been taken, however wild the comedy, to achieve an authentic background. Many shots have the look of the

Buster Keaton and THE GENERAL.

unavoidable Matthew Brady photographs, and the final scenes are treated with a realism unusual in a film of its kind.

Russia's *New Bablyon* (*Novy Babilon*, 1929, Grigori Kozintsev) deals with the Franco-Prussian war and the Paris Commune of 1870/71 in expressionist style, angled to agree with official ideology. The New Babylon of the title is a huge department store symbolising and epitomising the French capital.

Abel Gance's vast Napoleonic epic referred to previously traces only its hero's early days, stopping short at the Italian campaign—thus the later ignominious defeats are left veiled in the future. Though usually known as *Napoléon,* the full title is *Napoléon vu par Abel Gance,* which presumably serves to excuse the historic perversion. It is, in fact, very much an act of worship—even to the extent of encircling the revered head from time to time with a halo of light. "I began to wonder," remarked a contemporary critic, "if Cecil B. De-Mille's name had been inadvertently omitted from the programme."

A little-known and underrated film—now apparently vanished altogether—was the British *Bolibar* (1928, Walter Summers). Set in the time of the Peninsular War, it deals with the siege of the town of Bolibar, then in the hands of Napoleonic troops, by Spanish guerillas. Though no great masterpiece, and more concerned with the romantic activities of the besieged than with the military activities of the besiegers, it is in many ways an unusual and imaginative work, notable for the beauty both of its photography (by Jack Parker) and of its star, Elissa Landi. It was another victim of the imminent arrival of sound, and certainly does not deserve the complete oblivion into which it has sunk.

A dramatic still from I WAS A SPY.

42

4. Disillusion—
Then the Clouds Re-Gather

BY THE END of the Twenties and the advent of the talking picture, the general disenchantment with war had seeped through to the makers of films. It received its first notable expression in Lewis Milestone's *All Quiet on the Western Front* (1930, adapted from Erich Maria Remarque's best-selling novel), still generally regarded as one of the greatest of all anti-war films. In the climate of the times its success was assured—though it was not welcomed with particularly wide-open arms in certain European countries. It was, as suggested earlier, an opportune rather than a "courageous" venture, and it made a great deal of money, being reissued later in another safe period, the Fifties. Technically, and allowing for the unavoidably primitive quality of the sound, it contains much that can still be admired. The wide-sweeping battle sequences are impressive and terrifying in their din and confusion, and symbolic scenes such as that in the schoolroom still make their point. The famous shot at the close, where the boy's hand (said, in fact, to be that of the director himself) reaches out from the trench for the butterfly and is suddenly convulsed in death from a sniper's bullet, is emotionally moving but intellectually confused when regarded as symbolism. Symbolic of what? Young soldiers at war, particularly after the shattering experiences undergone by this particular boy, are not generally inclined to grasp at fragile beauty from the filth of their surroundings. It was, in addition, a chance moment, and symbolism and chance do not blend well. Young Paul, the soldier in question, undoubtedly cold and hungry, would have been as likely to have been shot reaching out for a discarded can of beans. The most interesting aspect of all (and perhaps one not wholly foreseen) resulted from the casting of such obvious young Americans as young Germans. The viewer's sense of nationalism is at once confused, so that all awareness of two sides at war becomes blurred and the group of young men becomes, as it were, an amalgam of friend and enemy—each individual a conjoined unit of mutual suffering.

Lew Ayres and Raymond Griffith in the famous shell-hole sequence from ALL QUIET ON THE WESTERN FRONT.

Undeniably *All Quiet* relentlessly exposes "the tragedy and futility of war" (or, at any rate, of that particular war concluded sufficiently long ago for disillusion to have set in), but one is left with a slightly uneasy feeling that everything is neatly timed to cash in—a feeling seemingly justified by the director's later career. Not very many years afterwards Milestone was making films as bellicose as any, retaining from *All Quiet* only a certain sympathy for the individual soldier's plight. A film director has, of course, as much right as anyone else to change his mind, but knowing what is to follow cannot but affect one's view of the earlier work. It suggests an attitude encountered with depressing monotony in the cinema—past wars were damnable, disgraceful, and unnecessary, but the contemporary one is always "just."

Though falling short of Arnold Zweig's powerful book, another 1930 film from America, *The Case of Sergeant Grischa,* a condemnation of military indifference to justice, is not without its cogent moments, reinforced by the strength of Chester Morris's performance. Perhaps, however, Herbert Brenon, director of the fine *War Brides,* was of too gentle a disposition for the ruthless subject.

44

Appearing in the same year as *All Quiet,* and often regarded as almost a companion piece, was G. W. Pabst's *Westfront 1918,* Germany's chief contribution to disillusion. Slow, sombre, weighty, deliberately monotonous, concentrating on the barren, ruined landscapes of trench warfare, it evokes an atmosphere of leaden desolation, sometimes confusing, and not altogether avoiding the pitfall of becoming boring when trying to represent boredom. It is, nonetheless, an impressive and moving indictment. Nazi Germany liked it not at all.

Another significant work in an unusually good year was *Journey's End,* directed by James Whale and made in America largely owing to the lack of adequate sound equipment in Britain. The script was adapted from R. C. Sherriff's famous play about the effect of war on the ordinary men despatched to wage it, and Whale had the intelligence to keep the scenario very close to the theatre to which it belonged, thus preserving Colin Clive's magnificent performance in its proper perspective.

Comparing interestingly with the above is Anthony Asquith's *Tell*

A lighter moment from Pabst's WESTFRONT 1918.

Colin Clive (right) in JOURNEY'S END.

TELL ENGLAND, directed by Anthony Asquith.

46

England (1931). The outlook is similar—so is the class structure: disillusioned officer types, loyal and/or comic serving men. To some extent *Tell England* sacrifices character to spectacle, and it also slips, where *Journey's End* manages not to, into moments of uneasy sentimentality. The Gallipoli landing scenes, however, are magnificently handled, leaving the spectator depressingly aware of the criminal futility of the whole botched campaign. Without oratory, both films are eloquent about the utter waste, the wanton expenditure of the lives of men.

Throughout the period the conventional sob-operas continued to appear. Frank Borzage directed Helen Hayes and Gary Cooper in Ernest Hemingway's *A Farewell to Arms* (1932) —to be remade by Charles Vidor in 1957 with Rock Hudson and Jennifer Jones. Victor Fleming was responsible for a third version of *The White Sister.*

Straightforward adventure tales came from Britain: *The W Plan* (1930) and *I Was a Spy* (1933), both from Victor Saville, expertly tailored, smoothly played, easily forgotten. Germany was praised in America for the absence of nationalistic hatred in the submarine film *Morgenrot* (1933, Gustav Ucicky), released the day after Hitler became Reich Chancellor, and also sent over *Hell on Earth* (*Niemandsland*, 1931, Victor Trivas) and *The Doomed Battalion* (*Berge in Flammen*, 1931, Luis Trenker), demonstrating how personal friendships can transcend national prejudices. Oddities included Joan Blondell singing of her Forgotten Man in the lavish musical *Gold-Diggers of 1933,* as queues of depression-starved beggars were contrasted with tableaux of men in the army uniforms of fifteen years earlier.

Aerial films reached a climax with the spectacular *Hell's Angels* (1930, Howard Hughes). Apart from its sheer size and a few exciting sequences—such as a Zeppelin raid, an attack on an ammunition dump, and a foretaste of the sky battles to become so stupefyingly stereotyped in the Second World War—it had little to offer and virtually nothing to say, being based on a story of surpassing silliness that makes *Wings* look almost intelligent. The film started out as a silent and had to be hurriedly embellished with dialogue sequences *en route,* necessitating the replacement of the beautiful and accomplished Swedish actress Greta Nissen by Jean Harlow. Less grandiose and more interesting was the first version of *The Dawn Patrol* (1930, Howard Hawks), which at least contained some pointed dialogue and three-dimensional characters. The 1938 remake (directed by Edmund Goulding), unscrupulously wrenched into a pro-war shape, was less worthy, despite ingratiating performances from David Niven and Errol Flynn. Other air war films of the early Thirties included *The Eagle*

47

and the Hawk (1933, Stuart Walker) *Sky Devils* (1932, Edward Sutherland) with Spencer Tracy, and *Ace of Aces* (1933, J. W. Ruben). The last of these is the most noteworthy, demonstrating the brutalising effect of war on a young sculptor (Richard Dix at his best) who is first scorned by his wife because of his objection to joining in the fighting and then, when he submits and returns as a famous flyer, spurned by her because of his coarseness.

Of all the war films of these years, however, the most powerful, and most undervalued, is Ernst Lubitsch's *The Man I Killed* (1932, degraded by the ludicrous alternative title *Broken Lullaby*), telling the story of a young Frenchman who goes to Germany after the Armistice to ask forgiveness from the family of a soldier whom he bayonetted to death. In later years this film has been accused of indulging in melodramatics: this was certainly not regarded as true at the time. It was, in fact, too deeply disturbing for comfort, and failed at the box office. Nevertheless, in respect of any other consideration apart from financial return, it would need all Lubitsch's brilliant comedies placed together in the scales to level them against this, his

Victory parade: Lubitsch's THE MAN I KILLED.

Phillips Holmes and Nancy Carroll in THE MAN I KILLED.

one serious film. In the early part there are a few brief scenes of the conclusion of hostilities: the camera passes slowly over the gleaming swords and accoutrements of the top brass kneeling at a thanksgiving service; a victory parade is viewed through the open space left by the amputated leg of a watching soldier; a roar of cannon celebrating peace causes a shattered man in a hospital bed to awake shrieking in terror. In short moments such as these Lubitsch says, concisely and devastatingly, all that need be said about the trappings and hypocrisy of peace with honour, and the ghastly union of Church and Military. Ironically, Phillips Holmes, criticised as ineffective in portraying the young Frenchman, was killed in the war that films such as this failed to avert.

*   *   *

With the arrival of the mid-Thirties the climate began to change. As war clouds gathered, most film-makers made haste to put up their little umbrellas; with notable celerity they changed the pipe of peace for the martial trumpet. Exactly half-way through the decade appeared

49

Walter Forde's *Brown on Resolution* (American title: *Forever England*), based on a novel by C. S. Forester. The moral implications of this film (made with "the full approval of the Admiralty") are so dubious that one cannot help wondering whether its makers were really aware of what they were saying. Set in the First World War, it tells of a young able seaman who is rescued by the Germans when his ship is sunk in action, and later repays his rescuers by sniping at them and thus delaying repairs to their own ship until that too is sunk. The sailor, played by John Mills in his first starring role, is displayed for our admiration, but in fact the film would appear to convey a sharp warning—"Leave your enemies to drown or they'll end up drowning you." The film was among those shown to the Civil Defence and First Aid Posts to while away the long hours between raids. What they were supposed to learn from it was not clear, but it certainly leaves an odd taste in the mouth. In 1953 it was dusted off and updated to fit the Second World War.

Bright little comedies appeared from both America and Britain, with such titles as *Sons o' Guns* (1936, Lloyd Bacon). Exciting adventures like *Submarine Patrol* (1938, John Ford), *O.H.M.S.* (1936, Raoul Walsh), *Pride of the Navy* (1939, Charles Lamont) and the death-or-glory *Charge of the Light Brigade* (1936, Michael Curtiz) — all vengeance and Errol Flynn—extolled to a greater or lesser degree the delights and thrills of a fighter's life, and began to replace the anti-war productions. Even a fundamentally pacifist film like Howard Hawks's *Road to Glory* (1936) had to be injected with shots of chauvinist propaganda; even a straight-forward thriller like Hitchcock's *The Lady Vanishes* (1938) had to have its pacifist who is proved to be a misguided fool and ultimately loses his life.

"Watch-out!" films began to reappear. As early as 1929 the Gaumont sound feature *High Tension* (Maurice Elvey), a much derided picture, had foretold the bombing of Peace Missions by unscrupulous agents in 1940. Now in 1938, the tone was changed and such destruction would presumably have been lauded as a patriotic act. *Midnight Menace* (1937, Sinclair Hill) concerned an international plot to bomb London by night: the chief villain was known as a mythical "Minister for Grovinia," but was played by the unmistakably German actor Fritz Kortner. *Things to Come* (1935, William Cameron Menzies) opened with a terrifying prediction of massed bombers advancing over the coast of London at the outbreak of an undeclared war—the most effective sequence in the whole of this Wellsian vision of the future. Incredibly, even that hoary old melodrama by Guy du Maurier ("A Patriot") entitled *An Englishman's Home* was brought up to date (enemy plane drops parachute troops to take possession of Mr. Brown's country house and transmit wireless information), as a grim warning against unpreparedness. The director was Albert de Courville and its appearance coincided almost exactly with the outbreak of the Second World War. Meanwhile admonitory films such as *Confessions of a Nazi Spy* (1939, Anatole Litvak) kept the pot boiling in America.

There were, naturally, left-overs from the peaceable years. *They Gave Him a Gun* (1937, W. S. Van Dyke, with Spencer Tracy) takes as its theme that if you knock the gentleness out of a man and put a gun in his hand he may end up by using it for his own purposes rather than yours. *Idiot's Delight* (1939, Clarence Brown), though greatly weakened from the original play, still retains a little of its mordancy. James Whale's *The Road Back* (1937), from Erich Maria Remarque's novel, is one of his less successful ventures, but deals with considerable insight and sympathy with the problems of German soldiers struggling to exist in the aftermath of 1918.

From France came *La kermesse héroïque* (1936, Jacques Feyder), charmingly and wittily expounding the theme of the open city in the Sixteenth century. The men of a quiet Flemish town that is threatened by the Spanish governor of Flanders shiver with apprehension at the thought of imminent slaughter and rapine. Their womenfolk, however, under the command of the Mayor's wife (enchantingly played by Françoise Rosay) decide to welcome the invaders with, if necessary, literally open arms and thus, in more senses than one, disarm them. In view of what was to happen in a few years time, this suggestion of "if rape is inevitable relax and enjoy it" acquired a somewhat sour taste. Indeed, the film was looked on as one of the most significant productions of its year—by Nazi Germany. *Au service de la France* (Raymond Bernard, starring Edwige Feuillère and Erich von Stroheim) though basically a spy melodrama, emphasised the misery and suffering of war, and particularly its aftermath—an aspect studiously ignored by most pro-war productions. In *Les otages* (*The Hostages,* 1939, by the same director) the unwilling volunteers who, in order to save their village from destruction, offer themselves to the enemy to be shot unless the murderer of a German officer is discovered, are depicted as far from heroic characters. Their captors are treated as equally human and the whole business—a sidestream of war—is presented with gentle irony. In 1937 Abel Gance re-made his *J'accuse* as a sound feature.

The most important French film of the period was Jean Renoir's *La grande illusion* (1937). The main events take place in a prisoner-

of-war camp set in an old castle and run by the aristocratic Commandant, von Rauffenstein (Erich von Stroheim). Based on Renoir's
own experiences, the story traces the respect and sympathy that develops between the Commandant and one of his prisoners, a cultured
young officer named Boildieu (Pierre Fresnay). Together with the
bourgeois Maréchal (Jean Gabin), Boildieu had earlier been shot
down by von Rauffenstein, then an air ace, and entertained by him
to dinner as a brother officer. Later, after various adventures, the two
Frenchmen landed up at the castle, and there met up again with von
Rauffenstein who had meanwhile been severely wounded. The sense
of understanding between the two aristocrats, based on mutual values,
is echoed by the companionship that developes between the "ordinary"
soldiers—of both sides. Maréchal plans an escape with a rich and
fervently patriotic Jew. Boildieu helps them, but in doing so places
himself deliberately in a position where he has to be shot down by
the Commandant. The Frenchman dies, in a deeply affecting scene,
with the German watching by his bedside, both realising they belong
to a world—and a code of conduct—fast vanishing for ever. We follow
the further adventures of the two who escaped, but it is the relationship between Boildieu and von Rauffenstein, and the earlier relationship between Boildieu and Maréchal, that are at the heart of
the film. Maréchal remarks to Rosenthal, the Jew, that despite his
closeness to Boildieu there has always been a strange barrier between
them. National barriers are more artificial than those of class. Renoir
handles his material brilliantly, drawing impeccable performances
from Jean Gabin, Fresnay and von Stroheim. The high surgical collar
which von Rauffenstein is forced to wear after his wound is an inspired touch—satirising the unbending stiffness of the Prussian mili-
tarist type, yet suggesting that it is removable (or in time will be)
and even that it was originally imposed by injury. The quiet, un-
obtrusive style of the whole film adds immensely to its power. It
could be regarded as a last despairing plea—to friend and enemy alike—
to draw back from the abyss towards which each was galloping. Certainly it was recognised as such by the Nazis. It was banned in Germany, and Mussolini was persuaded to influence the Venice Film
Festival adversely in their attitude towards it. *La grande illusion* is a
film of, as well as about, nobility, one of the last anti-war pictures
in which the pervading emotion is one of profound, compassionate
grief rather than sick, lacerating bitterness.

* * *

Among films of other wars, two of the most memorable were America's *Blockade* and Russia's *Alexander Nevsky* (*Alexandr Nyevski*). The latter (1938, Sergey Eisenstein, with music by Prokofiev) is a historical spectacular created in a spirit of patriotic pageantry, having as its climax the defeat of the Teutonic Knights in 1242 by the Russians under Grand Duke Alexander Nevsky. The battle, which took place on the ice-covered Lake Preipus, may be regarded as a great paean to violence—for the very best of reasons. There is no denying that the clash of combat has rarely been more strikingly photographed: visually satisfying and emotionally exciting though it is, however, there is little more to it than this. The Teutons are villains to the last tin-clothed man; the Russians, grave or carefree, dignified or comic, are heroes one and all. As a study of black versus white, it comes through with flying colours, and modern parallels are strongly implied. The production caused some faces to redden when the Soviet-German Pact was signed, and was relegated to a shelf until the lunatic shiftings of power agreements enabled it to be dusted off and taken down.

The terrible civil war in Spain brought forth surprisingly few contemporary films, the only fictional one of note being *Blockade* (1938, William Dieterle, with Henry Fonda and Madeleine Carroll). Though built on a melodramatic—indeed, an operatic—spy story, and discreet even to the point of avoiding identification of the opposing sides, there is a refreshing sincerity in this minor but unexceptionable work. Explicit or not, there is no doubt as to where its sympathies lie: later, after official sympathy on world ideologies had shifted back and forth several times, its author, John Howard Lawson, was to be penalised as one of the Hollywood Ten.

A remarkable documentary on the same conflict was *The Spanish Earth* (1937) made by Joris Ivens with a commentary by Ernest Hemingway. Ivens went to Spain for the specific purpose of making a film for the support of the Republican forces, and had intended to use a compilation of newsreels. Ultimately, however, a dramatic synopsis was drawn up following the progress of a deliberately anonymous and unremarkable young man from his humble village to the fighting in Madrid. It is declared propaganda, closing with the favoured side apparently in triumph, with no suggestion of what was to follow. Other documentaries from Britain and America were *Heart of Spain* (1937, Herbert Kline), *Spain* (1939, a compilation film edited by Esther Shub) and *Spanish ABC* (1938, Thorold Dickinson). The only film made by the novelist André Malraux had the war as its subject: entitled *L'espoir* (*Days of Hope*, 1938) and based on his novel of the same name, it tells its story in a formal, stylised, episodic

53

manner that somewhat detracts from the realism of its subject.

All the above viewed the struggle from the Republican side. Across the way was Augusto Genina's *L'assedio dell' Alcázar,* a strident but undeniably competent piece of pro-Franco propaganda, in the course of which Henry Fonda's declaration at the end of *Blockade,* "This isn't war—it's murder," is neatly echoed by a character on the opposing side. From either party the remark is meaningless, and has been hurled as a term of abuse in all conflicts since the beginning of time.

A costly pomposity from Italy was Carmine Gallone's *Scipio Africanus* (1937) which starred Isa Miranda. The famous Roman general's exploits were squeezed into fantastic shapes to equate them to those of Mussolini. The attack on Abyssinia also gave rise to a number of films that do not appear to have travelled very far beyond their place of origin.

5. The Second World War

THAT THE SECOND WORLD WAR saw the Great Resurgence of British Cinema is now a truism that needs no emphasising. It started off, however, with a real clanger. *The Lion Has Wings* (1939, Michael Powell, Brian Desmond Hurst, Adrian Brunel) was a fictionalised documentary with a lengthy climax demonstrating the unassailability of Britain's air defences. It was intended "to inspire quiet confidence in the hearts of those who saw it." What it more probably did inspire was the blush of embarrassment as, a year or so later, filmmakers and audience crouched together in their bomb-shaken underground shelters.

By 1941, however, films were appearing that caught with remarkable accuracy the mood of the moment—a mixture of glum acceptance and grim determination—and the test of their honesty is that they can be seen today, or most of them, without that uncomfortable sense of expediency caused by so much out-of-date propaganda. Facts were faced, heroics were "out," the enemy were represented neither as wooden-headed dolts or monstrous villains. In four major films a British battleship is sunk, a group of British soldiers are last seen— after arduous training—on their way to almost certain death, a little "careless talk" leads to a raid costing appalling casualties, and an entire community is hoodwinked and rendered helpless by a handful of resourceful German parachute troops. The threat of disaster, indeed, is faced almost with relish. On more than one occasion a Nazi is cleverer (and more interesting) than the Allies he encounters, even though he must be beaten in the end.

The latter situation occurs in *49th Parallel* (*The Invaders*, 1941, Michael Powell), an excellently told adventure story—no less but no more—about a group of Germans landed by submarine in Canada. It was the first of the many. Powell followed it up in 1942 with *One of Our Aircraft Is Missing*, which opens in realistic fashion with the briefing (spoken by the director himself) and execution of a bombing raid, but develops into a straightforward suspense tale when a

The betrayed landing: Thorold Dickinson's NEXT OF KIN.

crew is forced to bail out and has to escape from occupied Holland. Pamela Brown, Googie Withers, Peter Ustinov and other familiar British faces appear somewhat incongruously (but reassuringly) in the Dutch landscape to help the lads on their way, and the film closes with "we'll-be-back" undertones that were to be whispered again during the coming months.

Next of Kin (1941, Thorold Dickinson), the anti-careless talk production referred to above, was originally made as a cautionary tale to impress HM Forces, but it was later released, with great and unexpected success, to the general public. Even now, when careless talk is the order of the day, it grips the interest, despite some crudely artificial settings, as a simple spy story. In its time it was quite effective propaganda, made notable by Mervyn Johns's chillingly commonplace informer.

A true incident is commemorated in *The Foreman Went to France* (1942), a meritorious second film by a young former editor, Charles Frend. After the fall of France a works foreman crosses the English

IN WHICH WE SERVE

STARRING

NOEL COWARD   JOHN MILLS
BERNARD MILES CELIA JOHNSON
JOYCE CAREY   KAY WALSH

G.F.D. RELEASE   CERTIFICATE U

Nöel Coward in his own film IN WHICH WE SERVE.

Channel determined to retrieve some vital equipment. It is quietly stir-
ring stuff, well calculated to appeal to the love of "rugged individual-
ism" supposedly held by the British before it was drained away by the
politicians, planners, panderers and pamperers of the post-war and
succeeding decades. France being at the time out of bounds for British
film producers, the countryside was adequately represented by Corn-
wall.

The most famous production of 1942 was undoubtedly *In Which
We Serve,* written, directed and starred in by Noël Coward, who also
composed the music. Inspired by the sinking of HMS Kelly off Crete,
the story follows the life of a destroyer from the time of her building
to her last fatal encounter. It is told in a long flashback as the Captain
and members of the crew cling to a raft in the oil-muddied water,
with further brief flashbacks into the personal lives of the men.
Though it has been condemned as the "apotheosis of the stiff upper
lip" by those to whom the drooling lower lip seems preferable, it is
in truth a warm, compassionate and totally unsnobbish study of a

group of men—and women—gathered from various walks of life and united by a common devotion. Admittedly suited to the mood of the moment, admittedly simplifying both attitudes and motives, the film interests today as history, but it can still move deeply as purely human drama. The long, slow final scene, where the Captain shakes hands with each surviving member of the crew of his lost ship can sound embarrassingly sentimental in description—in actuality it is handled

The "Royal Engineers" take over the village: a tense scene from WENT THE DAY WELL?

with such restraint and dignity, and with so subtle a suggestion of the unseen presence of those who drowned, that it remains as poignant a moment as any in the cinema. Only in the brief episode of the sailor who allows his fears to show (a part so well played by Richard Attenborough that he was condemned to similar characters for a long time ahead) does the film let itself down—with a "holier-than-thou" attitude, a smug lack of understanding of human failing under extreme stress, that is out of key with the rest. The nastier side of propaganda peeps briefly through.

In two smaller-scaled productions Leslie Howard directed and demonstrated his own quiet charm—*Pimpernel Smith* (1941) and *The First of the Few* (*Spitfire*, 1942). The first is a simple spy-and-escape drama, the star portraying a modern absent-minded-professor version of Sir Percy Blakeney and smuggling desirable characters out of the hands of the Gestapo, closing with the famous whispered phrase "I shall be back—we shall all be back." It is one of the few serious films of the period to contain a wooden-headed enemy caricature—played with disarming gusto by Francis L. Sullivan. *The First of the Few*, a low-keyed, unpretentious account of the invention of the famous Spitfire plane, is given an added touch of tragic irony by Howard's sympathetic performance—his beautifully played death scene so soon to be followed by the reality of his own. He was killed in a plane destroyed by enemy action the following year.

One of the strangest productions of the entire war was the underrated *Went the Day Well?* (1942, the first full-length British picture directed by Alberto Cavalcanti). Based on a story by Graham Greene, it views with a coldly appraising eye what could happen in the event of a surprise small-scale German landing. The inhabitants of a remote village are surprised by the arrival of a company of "Royal Engineers"—but dutifully billet them and make them welcome. Once the troops are installed they reveal themselves as German parachutists, and very quickly render the entire community powerless. Despite all the official warnings and advice they have been receiving, the villagers are unable to move, and one attempt after another to raise the alarm is thwarted. Predictably, rescue arrives at last, but not until a good many lessons have been learnt. The village characters are deliberately stereotyped, and their village deliberately "typical"—they and it are meant as models not individuals, and to dismiss them as banal (which was done in one instance) is to miss the whole point. Even though it was intended as a *Next of Kin*-type warning, a film of this frankness, with its uncompromising acceptance of the possibility of defeat, would have been unthinkable during the First World War. The closer the

59

Attack: from SHIPS WITH WINGS.

danger, it seems, the stronger the grasp (in the film world) on reality.

Underneath this superior crust bubbled the usual pot-boilers, seasoned with whatever propagandist flavour appeared to suit time and circumstance. Spy and adventure dramas such as *Bulldog Sees It Through* (1940, Harold Huth), *Dangerous Moonlight* (1941, Brian Desmond Hurst), *Ships with Wings* (1941, Sergey Nolbandov), *Freedom Radio* (1941, Anthony Asquith), *The Day Will Dawn* (1942, Harold French), *Secret Mission* (1942, Harold French), *Salute John Citizen* (1942, Maurice Elvey) strained credulity to varying lengths. "Comedies" of the sort indicated by such titles as *Gert and Daisy Clean Up* (1942, Maclean Rogers), *Back-Room Boy* (1942, Herbert Mason, with Arthur Askey), *Warn That Man* (1943, Lawrence Huntington) and *Old Bill and Son* (1940, Ian Dalrymple), a feeble updating with none of the salty cynicism of the Bairnsfather characters, were added depressants to the grim miseries of wartime Britain.

The Gentle Sex (1943, Leslie Howard) and *Millions Like Us* (1943, Frank Launder and Sidney Gilliat) dealt with the war from the feminine angle. The first concerns a group of girls from varying backgrounds coming together in the ATS, the second concerns a group of girls from varying backgrounds coming together in a munitions factory. Either, without much adjustment, could have come from the pages of the same wartime women's magazine.

The British documentary short proceeded with commendable speed and quality: *The First Days,* produced by the GPO Unit under Cavalcanti and appearing in 1939, is a 23-minute record of the period immediately following the declaration of war—inevitably intent on engendering the "cheerful fortitude" atmosphere, but without forcing things too unacceptably. *Target for Tonight* (1941, Harry Watt) follows the progress of a single bomber taking part in a raid over Germany. *Coastal Command* (1942, J. B. Holmes) is concerned with the co-operation between Navy and shore-based aircraft to ensure the safe conduct of convoys. Both seemed splendid at the time—perhaps a little less so now, having been overtaken by the great strides in the *genre* since. Despite its opposing array of well-wishers *The Big Blockade* (1942, Charles Frend, with the "fullest co-operation" of Ministry of Economic Warfare and help from the Royal Navy, the War Office and the RAF) is a somewhat naively optimistic dramatised documentary on how Hitler would be blockaded into surrender.

The *doyen* of the war documentary of these years was without

Standing by for the blitz: Humphrey Jennings's LONDON CAN TAKE IT.

doubt Humphrey Jennings, who managed uniquely to transform his factual material into poetry with a quality all its own. He worked with Harry Watt and Pat Jackson on Cavalcanti's *The First Days*, referred to in the preceding paragraph, and in 1940 made *London Can Take It* (again with Harry Watt, for the Ministry of Information through the GPO Unit)—a 10-minute account of the first night of the London air raids in the form of a despatch by the American correspondent, Quentin Reynolds. Together with Jennings's *Fires Were Started* (1943) and to a lesser extent Basil Dearden's semi-documentary *The Bells Go Down* (1943) these are almost the only accurate scenes of the Blitz—except possibly for one brief moment from *In Which We Serve*. The atmosphere of those battered days and nights seems to have eluded feature film-makers with surprising entirety. Hitchcock made a bad shot at it (admittedly from several thousand miles away) in *Foreign Correspondent* (1940); the Blitz scenes were much the least convincing part of the mammoth post-war spectacular *Battle of Britain* (1969); and Walter Pidgeon, taking a leaf out of *Journey's End* and reading from "Alice in Wonderland" to his cosily tucked-up children in their cosy Miniver shelter, may have been well-intentioned but must have raised many a twisted smile on the faces of a large number of people as they crouched in their squalid, cramped, damp burrows. Where, for instance, did all that gentle light come from which so ravishingly illuminated Mrs. Miniver's clean radiant face and beautifully untroubled hair? (See page 65 for further comments on *Mrs. Miniver*)

Jennings continued with *Spring Offensive* (1940), *Heart of Britain* (1941) and *Words for Battle* (1941). *Listen to Britain*, which he made with Stewart McAllister the same year, is a wartime tone poem, weaving the music of Forces orchestras and Myra Hess playing at National Gallery concerts, together with dance hall songs, marching feet, tanks, planes and ordnance factories into a brilliant sound-and-vision mosaic. *Fires Were Started*, mentioned above, is a reconstruction of a single night's activity in an Auxiliary Fire Station. *The Silent Village* (1943) told the story of the destruction of the Czechoslovakian Lidice as it might have happened in a Welsh mining valley. *The Eighty Days* and *VI* followed in 1944, and the following year saw the production of *A Diary for Timothy*, using a new-born baby as a vague symbol of transition from war to a strange and unimaginable "peace." The tone here is pessimistic, Jennings making no secret of his fears concerning the effect that years of war, propaganda and the instillation of wartime values might have on the moral and physical welfare of peoples about to face the most difficult of all tasks—the reconstruction of a

Two scenes from the blitz: above—*FIRES WERE STARTED (Humphrey Jennings); below—THE BELLS GO DOWN (Basil Dearden).*

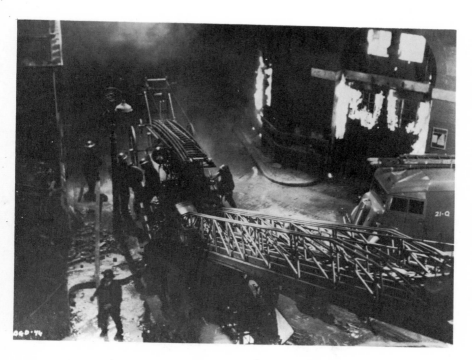

broken world and a discredited way of life. Jennings died in 1950, still comparatively young, the lyric poet of the war on film.

*   *   *

Before turning to Pearl Harbor, the war in the desert, and all that was to follow, we may glance briefly at the American war film scene before she herself became involved. The work that swamped the screens of the period was the Civil War epic *Gone with the Wind* (1939, mostly by Victor Fleming, with additional work by George Cukor and Sam Wood). It is only incidentally a "war picture," using the great gash across America's history as background and support to a story that might reasonably be described as aristocratic-novelette. Even so, the huge panoramas of destruction, the burning of Atlanta, the multitude of wounded and dying, the panic and misery of flight, the loss of all moral values and integrity in the desolation of aftermath, are all impressively horrifying. The mammoth movie presents vividly, if it says little.

The First World War was still being quarried, yielding such gems as *Enemy Agent* (1939, Terry Morse) with Boris Karloff as a spy,

The famous panorama of the wounded at the Atlanta railroad from GONE WITH THE WIND.

and *We're in the Army Now* (1939, H. B. Humberstone) featuring the Ritz Brothers. Howard Hawks directed *Sergeant York* (1941), the story, based on fact, of a religious Tennessee farmer who registers his conscientious objection to war, is persuaded by an army major to discard his scruples (he is given an American history book to help him to do so), goes to war, and ends up killing twenty-five of the enemy and capturing more. He thus qualifies as a hero. Gary Cooper made effective use of his "worried" look (and no wonder) and was awarded an Academy Award for it. The real Sergeant York, on being asked what he thought of the film and its portrayal of himself, is reported to have said, after a ruminative pause, "very natural." The film made a great deal of money. Its timing may have been fortuitous, maybe not.

This above All (1942, Anatole Litvak) is another study of conversion, this time of a deserter after Dunkirk who meets up with a WAAF. Love restores his faith in war, and he goes to give himself up to the authorities, but is caught up in an air raid on the way, rescues a woman and child from a burning building, and ends up in hospital. There he marries his WAAF and realises the importance of being true to thine own self. The motivation is as hard to accept as the details of "English" people and places.

Mystery Sea Raider (1940, Edward Dmytryk), apparently inspired by the sinking of *Athenia,* tells the adventures of a girl torpedoed on her way from England to America and later suspected of treachery. In *A Yank in the RAF* (1941, Henry King) Tyrone Power takes part in the Dunkirk evacuation and is rewarded with Betty Grable. *Women in War* is a glossy magazine story of the Overseas Nursing Corps in France. The list could be extended indefinitely: they are no more puerile than their British counterparts and presumably kept the studios ticking over until better opportunities might be expected to arise.

Mrs. Miniver (1942, William Wyler), described as a "tribute to the British and their courage in the hour of ordeal," presents a picture of their country life that must have astounded village folk up and down the land. There is one genuinely moving sequence—the voyage of the "little boats" to Dunkirk—a moment of history that could hardly fail to be effective. For the rest, this is a doubtless kindly-intentioned (and extremely profitable) super-shiny romantic magazine story of the effect of the war on comfortable civilian life. It gleams so brightly, in fact, that even the dirt and grime, when they come, somehow look superficial and easily washed off. The final sequence is in the bombed (but still surprisingly clean) village church, with bright sunshine pouring warmly through the damaged roof. The parson preaches

Christianity and the congregation sing to the Lord while overhead roar British planes on their way to do unto others what they don't want done unto them. Treated with savage irony this could have been a strikingly effective close; unfortunately, it is all too solemnly meant, and the result is somewhat nauseating.

Lubitsch's *To Be or Not to Be* (1942), a satirical comedy about a group of actors caught in the destruction of Warsaw in 1939, led to the director being accused of bad taste in making fun of another country's sufferings. He indignantly denied this, and indeed the "fun" is made of the conquerors rather than the temporarily conquered. The Nazis are represented as pompous, strutting half-wits, but in a way totally different from the "serious caricaturing" of the enemy in the conventional war film. Even so, one is left with the feeling that such a film could only have been made very many miles from the homes of those who had experienced the activities of the half-wits, whether in Warsaw, Rotterdam, the little towns of invaded France, or in London.

* * *

With Pearl Harbor ensconced in history, John Farrow's *Wake Island* (1942) set the tone for the fairly worthless crop of feature war films to be issued from the United States during the next couple of years. "Based on authentic records" of the defence of the island against the Japanese in December 1941, it follows a monotonously similar pattern—moderately accurate backgrounds against which is played out a propagandist story of stock characters (or even worse, conscientiously eccentric characters) involved in situations of uninspiring predictability. *Parachute Nurse* (1942, Charles Barton) was aimed at recruitment in the American Women's Aerial Nursing Corps: be dropped by parachute to help patch up the wounded and you are likely to descend on romance (plus the excitement of an unscrupulous rival) as well. *Bombs over Burma* (1942, Joseph Lewis), *Air Force* (1942, Howard Hawks), *Flying Tigers* (1943, David Miller), *Five Graves to Cairo* (1943, Billy Wilder), *Bataan* (1943, Tay Garnett), *Destination Unknown* (1943, Ray Taylor), *Sahara* (1943, Zoltan Korda), *Wings over the Pacific* (1943, Phil Rosen), *A Wing and a Prayer* (1944, Henry Hathaway)—the Burma Road, the African desert, the Pacific, spies, troops, marines, airmen, each little film with its quota of embarrassing moments, its shot-in-the-arm patriotic sentiments, its regrettable necessity, its grim determination, its quips, its

66

cranks, its soft-centred toughness—that ubiquitous soft-centred toughness of the American war film! The spectacle of world-famous stars indulging in these antics results in the same sort of incredibility as the use of titled ladies to promote the use of a brand of toothpaste. The old, old familiar faces took the films one more step from reality while at the same time, presumably, increasing their propaganda value. Whatever the publicity hand-outs might say, these were commercial productions made to conform with the required attitude of the moment. Their expediency shines from them like the phosphorus on a decaying fish.

Even less edifying were atrocity pictures such as *Hitler's Children* (1943, Edward Dmytryk), protesting high moral indignation while drawing in the cash with sadistic scenes such as that of pretty Bonita Granville undergoing a flogging because she refuses to submit to the licentious Nazis.

Among the better productions of the period was *Immortal Sergeant* (1943, John Stahl), an interesting study of a tough sergeant and the effect on his men when he shoots himself to save them. The script, it should be noted, is from a British novel (by John Brophy) and about British soldiers—convincingly played by Thomas Mitchell and Henry Fonda. Hitchcock's *Lifeboat* (1943) is a dramatic allegory, the whole of which takes place in the boat of the title (and in a rather obvious tank): he ran into trouble from some quarters for making a Nazi the only character among the group of shipwrecked people to show much resourcefulness, despite the fact that he receives his deserts in the end. Cecil B. DeMille had his say with *The Story of Dr. Wassell,* an overblown, romanticised acount of the true adventures of an American doctor who smuggled a party of wounded soldiers from Java to safety in Australia. A simple tale of high courage is inflated into a grandiose Hollywood exhibition, Gary Cooper presiding.

Films such as the famed *Casablanca* (1942, Michael Curtiz) are on the perimeter of our subject—melodramatic thrillers rather than war films, but carefully angled to face the right way. Even in this thoroughly enjoyable tall story, for instance, there is one highly embarrassing and improbable scene when some German officers in a café start singing songs of the Fatherland, whereupon the customers, led by the band and an expatriate Czech, give vent to "La Marseillaise"—tear-stained female faces and all.

Lewis Milestone's *The Purple Heart* (1944) is a far cry indeed from *All Quiet on the Western Front,* the only thing in common being shrewd timing. *The Purple Heart* is merely an atrocity picture

67

directed against the Japanese. It gives a fictional account of a number of American airmen who are captured by the enemy and, when they refuse to answer questions, are threatened with torture and death. A Chinese traitor falsely accuses the men and is at once killed—in the courtroom—by his own son, whereupon the airmen, led by Dana Andrews, stand up in salutation of "a man." It is a sentiment of which any dictator would approve. Two years later Milestone made *A Walk in the Sun*—a study, not uninteresting at times, of a group of men in combat. No "realities of war" here—the whole film is seen, as it were, though a mist of literary contrivance. *Hitler's Madman* (1943, Douglas Sirk), America's version of the Lidice tragedy with John Carradine as Heydrich, is plodding and unimaginative, reducing a universal shame to the level of Grand Guignol.

As time passed, and victory grew more assured, an occasional film of greater worth appeared. *The Story of GI Joe* (1945, William Wellman), and *They Were Expendable* (1945, John Ford) are two of these. The first, a dramatised documentary based on the work of Ernie Pyle (played by Burgess Meredith) is sober, low-keyed, unhysterical, and almost totally convincing—demonstrating that you do not have to scream "war is hell" at the top of your voice in order to prove it so. *They Were Expendable* may not be Ford's best work, but it is well up in the list—a long, slow, never monotonous story of the early use of the combat PT boat, visually superb, and probably benefitting from the fact that, with success now appearing on the horizon, the facts of earlier failures could be squarely faced.

Thirty Seconds over Tokyo (1945, Mervyn LeRoy), deals in fairly conventional manner with a bomber on a mission of destruction over the Japanese capital. It eschews glory, laud and honour, and makes no bones about the horror of losing a leg—even in the service of the government of one's country. *Objective Burma* (1945, Raoul Walsh) is concerned with the retreat of a group of parachutists to their base after they have put a radar station out of action. It is a suspense story coldly reported, with Errol Flynn surprisingly free of swashbuckle. The coolness of the film itself was in odd contrast to the heat it engendered in some sensitive quarters on account of its alleged attempt to show that America (i.e. Flynn) was alone in winning the Far Eastern war. This seems rather an absurd accusation. The story deals with one small, isolated incident: making every allowance for the prevalence of her Allies there must have been occasional moments when the Americans had to get along as best they could on their own.

The above two offerings were a little better than might have been expected. *God Is My Co-Pilot* (1945, Robert Florey) was a good deal worse. During its dismal course a Catholic priest is seen reassuring a pilot—who is conscience-stricken by the fact that he has killed a large number of his fellow-men—that God is with him in the cockpit—that he is not to worry, every death means something to Him. This disgusting chit-chat, inserted into a conventional "autobiographical" adventure film, must surely bring Believer and Doubter together in a common nausea.

When it came to documentary, the United States output of the period showed up in somewhat brighter colours. The *Why We Fight* series, made with official support by Frank Capra, Anatole Litvak and others, may not have given very convincing answers to its questions, but at least it was—to use a contradiction in terms—honest propaganda: you knew what the makers were doing. There were seven films in the main series (1942–45): *Prelude to War, The Nazis Strike, Divide and Conquer, The Battle of Britain, The Battle of Russia* (a bit of an embarrassment, this, later on), *The Battle of China,* and *War Comes to America.* The general form is that of a documentary compilation— a form always conveniently lending itself to expedient distortions. Capra's *Battle of Britain* is probably the best of the bunch. This first series was followed by a *Know Your Enemy* and a *Know Your Ally* series, both cut short by the pressure of events. There was also an Anglo-American documentary, *Tunisian Victory* (1944), intended as a follow-up to the British *Desert Victory* but remaining some way behind in quality. Frank Capra had a large share in all these projects, and Dmitri Tiomkin was the universal composer. *Victory through Air Power* (1943), an animated historical lecture film purporting to demonstrate how long-range bombers could win the war, was made by Walt Disney with all the skill of *Snow White and the Seven Dwarfs.*

Most remarkable, though apparently generally seen in a mutilated version, is John Huston's *The Battle of San Pietro* (1944), a half-hour on-the-spot record of one infantry division's fight for a key Italian village. Huston also made *Report from the Aleutians* (1944) and much later, in 1948, *Let There Be Light,* a controversial and long-banned examination of the treatment of war neuroses.

*   *   *

As the tide of war slowly turned and the pace quickened, the number of noteworthy films from British sources understandably dwindled. Harry Watt's *Nine Men* (1943), his first feature film after a distinguished career in documentaries, ingeniously created the North

African desert in Wales. The film again deals with the old situation of an assorted group of people confined together, but lifted from the usual level by interesting characterisation and a really taut and intelligent script. Some concern was expressed at a later period over the film's attitude towards the Italians and the fact that one was shot while trying to escape, but it did not seem incongruous at the time.

Sometimes mistakenly described as a documentary, *San Demetrio, London* (1943, Charles Frend) is a fictional reconstruction of recent history, with professional actors and studio sets. It recounts, excitingly and without heroics, the story of the oil tanker that was set on fire and cut almost in two by shelling. Its crew, after drifting for three days in one of its boats, returned to the damaged ship, patched it up, and brought it safely to port. The production may be regarded as a "tribute" to the Merchant Navy, in line with *In Which We Serve* (Royal Navy), *The Way Ahead* (Army) and *The Way to the Stars* (Royal Air Force).

Carol Reed's *The Way Ahead* (1944) is one of the finest of all Second World War films. The formula is commonplace enough: a number of men from diverse occupations, classes and districts called

The battle to save the oil tanker: SAN DEMETRIO, LONDON.

Two more scenes from SAN DEMETRIO, LONDON.

William Hartnell as the sergeant; Raymond Huntley, John Laurie, Stanley Holloway and Jimmy Hanley as the raw recruits, in Carol Reed's fine tribute, THE WAY AHEAD.

up just after Dunkirk, trained, moulded into a homogeneous unit, and shipped off to the fighting in North Africa. Script, direction and performances combine together to conceal the artificiality of this well-worn formula. The characters may be types, but they are human beings we come to know, respect, and understand. The progress from the simulated and controllable danger of training to the unknown reality moves with superbly conveyed inevitability, reaching its climax in the long-awaited sound of the grinding menace of the approaching— but never clearly seen—enemy tanks. The final sequence, as the men we have come to know so well move individually through the enveloping dust—part of a group, perhaps, but in the last resort still vulnerable and alone—each grasping his little rifle against the heavy armour—is a high point in the entire output of war in the cinema. The film closes with the bravely prophetic title "The Beginning," but leaves us in little doubt as to whether these particular men will be there to see "The End." The scene has been interpreted as a plea for better armaments for the troops—very likely and very justified, but its significance is wider, and its effect longer-lasting, than any temporary purpose to be achieved.

In 1943 Anthony Asquith made *We Dive at Dawn,* another fictionalised documentary, this time about the sinking of a German battleship, the "Brandenburg" by the submarine "Sea Tiger." Well-trodden lines have been laid down by the script, and the director travels along them with evident discomfort. Much more representative is his Air Force film *The Way to the Stars (Johnny in the Clouds,* 1945). This is unusual in that it is to some extent a nostalgic look back to an earlier part of a war still in progress at the time of its making, and barely over at the time of its release. It opens with shots of a deserted, *débris*-spattered airfield in Britain, then moves back to the time when the place was humming with life—to tell the story of the men connected with it. Though another "group" film it attempts, in its restricted time, to delve deeper into character and motive than usual, concentrating more on personal problems than the general situation. Part of its purpose is to pay tribute to the Anglo-American co-operation that seemed—at the time—to be welding an indissoluble bond between the two nations. There is over the whole film an aura of melancholy strange for its time, when so much screen time was taken up with urging us all to smash our way through to the bright and brash future. It is, in fact, a lament for doomed youth everywhere, and bearing in mind that, though the war was clearly approaching its end while production was in progress, the film was actually in the cinemas by V-Day, it may well qualify as "courageous."

British documentary of the later war years included *Desert Victory* (1943) and *Burma Victory* (1945), both under the direction of Roy Boulting—skilfully edited compilations presenting in factual and easily assimilable form the complex events of the two campaigns. On a larger scale, *The True Glory* (1945, Carol Reed, Garson Kanin) does much the same for events from the Normandy invasion to the meeting across the Elbe; and *Theirs Is the Glory* (1946, Brian Desmond Hurst), a reconstruction made one year after the event, similarly covers the ill-fated Arnhem expedition. Despite the somewhat ambiguous effect caused by the juxtaposition of the two titles, the "glory" is meant to be shared, not claimed in rivalry.

*   *   *

As might be expected, war films from other countries were practically non-existent until the end of hostilities. Almost first in the

René Clément's *LA BATAILLE DU RAIL.*

field was René Clément's *La bataille du rail* (1943), a memorial to the activities of the French Resistance, and in particular the attacks on the trains, made in the style of contemporary newsreels. From Italy came the great trio of productions that, together with De Sica's *Shoe-Shine* (*Sciusià*, 1946) and *Bicycle Thieves* (*Ladri di biciclette*, 1948) brought neo-realism to the attention of the world: *Rome, Open City* (*Roma, città aperta*, 1945, Roberto Rossellini), *Paisà* (1946, Rossellini), and Luigi Zampa's *To Live in Peace* (*Vivere in pace*, 1946). *Rome, Open City,* though original in treatment, is conventional in outlook—patriotic defiance, courage under torture, etc. It was made in conditions of extreme difficulty and danger just prior to, and apparently in preparation for, the arrival of the Allies. The circumstances of its production, using cameras stolen from the Nazis, a script written partly in invisible ink, and photography snatched where and when an opportunity could be seized, give the film a rough finish that strengthens its impact.

In *Paisà,* however, a compilation of six short stories of varying quality dealing with the difficulties of adapting to the changing situations between peace and war, the poor photography and general

74

An intimate episode from Rossellini's portmanteau film, PAISÀ.

technical inadequacy has the appearance of a contrivance, and the shortcomings of some of the non-actors makes the "realism" considerably less real than the artificialities of the artist. Some of the stories, also, are such neatly shaped cameos that, better played and presented, they would almost have fitted into the Maugham Trios and Quartets of the Fifties.

Zampa's modest comedy-drama of the dilemma in which a quiet mountain village finds itself when two Americans seek refuge from the enemy has for too long been regarded as slighter than the others merely because it is lighter in tone. It is, however, one of the most sharply observed as well as entertaining war comedies.

A notable production from Switzerland was *The Last Chance* (1945, Leopold Lindtberg). Set in Italy after the fall of Mussolini, it deals with the escape of an American and two English soldiers and their efforts to lead a party of assorted refugees to Switzerland. Its theme of the essential brotherhood of men under threat is emphasised

75

by the variety of languages spoken by the party, and is implied rather than stated.

From Russia came *Natasha* (*Frontovyye podrugi,* 1942, V. Eisymont), *The Rainbow* (*Raduga,* 1944, Mark Donskoy), *No Greater Love* (*Ona zashchishchayet Rodinu,* 1944, Fridrikh Ermler), and documentaries such as *The Story of Stalingrad* (*Stalingrad,* 1943) and *Berlin* (1945). *The Rainbow* is the most striking of these, a grim horrifying picture of Nazis occupying a Ukrainian village, that no doubt most effectively sowed in all who saw it the proper seeds of retribution that were shortly to have so full and ghastly a flowering.

* * *

Earlier wars continued to receive barely a glance. Spain was accorded the full romantic treatment in Sam Wood's *For Whom the Bell Tolls* (1943), in which the personal concerns of Gary Cooper and Ingrid Bergman loom large against the strife. Adolph Zukor, who produced, is stated to have said "we are neither for nor against anyone," which was tactful, if slightly pallid.

Russia's *Kutuzov* (1944, Vladimir Petrov) draws the obvious parallels between Napoléon and Hitler in regard to the impregnability

A moment of tension from FOR WHOM THE BELL TOLLS.

76

More drama from FOR WHOM THE BELL TOLLS.

of Moscow, but was also an impressive spectacle apart from its propaganda values.

Agincourt was fought among the Welsh hills in Laurence Olivier's *Henry V* (1944), the bright colours of which illuminated the drab, rocket-ridden last months of the war. The pageantry and excitement of the great battle scene contrasts interestingly with the treatment of mediaeval conflict in the much later *Chimes at Midnight* (1966, Orson Welles), where the heavily armoured fighting men, with their banners and waving plumes, are slowly bogged down as they hack and hew at one another, into a morass of filth and mud, unrecognisable as friend or foe—or as human beings.

Panoply of (bygone) war: Olivier's HENRY V.

*'Human beings under duress': Michael Redgrave in THE CAPTIVE
HEART.*

6. Aftermath

APART FROM a few productions caught short by the cessation of hostilities, the screens of the early post-war years were, once again, more or less free of actual fighting films. Of the few that did appear the best was the British study of prisoners-of-war entitled *The Captive Heart* (1946, Basil Dearden), made in part at the Marlag Milag Nord Camp. Despite moments of embarrassing sentimentality the film is on the whole a moving account of human beings under duress, delving deeper into character and the effect of long imprisonment on both guards and victims than later pictures emphasising adventure and excitement but content to people the scene with cardboard figures. *A Bell for Adano* (1945, Henry King) is a restrained and often moving drama of reconstruction, set in a Sicilian town and built round the struggle by an American Major to overcome the suspicions of the inhabitants while working as Civil Affairs Administrator—a struggle symbolised and climaxed by the replacement of the town bell. King is seen here at his sensitive best.

For the rest there is not much to be said. *Tomorrow Is Forever* (U.S., 1945, Irving Pichel) is another woman's "glossy" using the World War—both World Wars, in fact—as convenient pegs on which to hang trite situations. A woman, worried about the idea of "giving" her American son to join in a European conflict, is persuaded to do so by her first husband (whom she does not recognise on his return from the 1914–18 war in which he was wounded)—and she thereupon despatches the young man—who was going to enlist in Canada anyway—with her best wishes. Both the director and such distinguished players as Orson Welles and Claudette Colbert deserved better material than this, mentioned here only as being typical of a certain type of war film frequently wasting screen time. *Tokyo Rose* (1946, Lew Landers) is an incredible farrago about an American prisoner-of-war in the hands of the Japanese who kidnaps a notorious female propagandist broadcaster. *Madame Pimpernel* (1946, Gregory Ratoff) achieves the unusual distinction of bringing together Constance Bennett and Gracie Fields in the same film and having no idea what to do with either of them. The unlikely pair help escaping British air-men from occupied Paris, kill a Gestapo agent, suffer torture, and are saved by the Liberation. Reputedly based on fact, it is a good example of how to make truth incredible.

The situation becomes brighter when we move from the war itself to its aftermath and the problems of rehabilitation. At least five films worthy of note came from the American or British studios. William Wyler's large-scale story of three ex-service men returning to civilian life in a small American town, *The Best Years of Our Lives* (1946, Sam Goldwyn's pinnacle) was probably over-praised at its appearance, and has certainly been over-condemned since. Smooth, shiny and sure-fire, it nevertheless tells its interwoven stories with skill and sympathy, avoiding bathos narrowly but with confidence. Even the courtship and marriage of the soldier who has lost both hands and has to struggle with a pair of steel claws (a situation which could easily have become as cheap a manipulation of an audience's emotions as the use of blindness to gain easy sympathy) are handled with a restraint, a form of off-hand dignity, that enables the watcher to feel unembarrassed at being moved. The chief interest of the film today may well lie in its preservation of a mood and atmosphere long dissipated.

Appearing several years after *The Best Years of Our Lives,* Fred Zinnemann's *The Men* (1950, from a script by Carl Foreman) deals honestly and clear-sightedly with the problems of paraplegics—war veterans who may have to spend the rest of their lives gravely incapacitated. Inevitably the film's scope is narrowed by having to concentrate on the story—the somewhat conventional story—of one man, played by the then unknown Marlon Brando. Even so, within the limits of its particularity this is an uncompromising picture, squarely facing such issues as the unlikelihood of any miraculous recovery of health and ability.

Fred Zinnemann was also responsible for the Swiss/American co-production *The Search* (*Die Gezeichneten,* 1947), about the plight of displaced European children without homes, families or future. The opening scenes, where the situation and outlook for the children is faced without fuss or emphasis, are remarkable. Thereafter the emotional appeal may seem somewhat facile—the scales, with so captivating a small boy as Ivan Jandl seated on them, somewhat loaded. Would a thoroughly unpleasant and vicious child, equally destroyed by war though he might be, have caused quite so many eyes to fill with tears? Allowing for this slight indulgence, however, the film strikes scarcely a single false note, except in the unnecessary intrusive

80

Displaced children in THE SEARCH, Fred Zinnemann's moving study of the innocent victims.

commentator who maddeningly indicates to us what we should be feeling at any particular moment. Perhaps, too, the American panacea is rather too unquestioningly assumed. Nevertheless, after years of strident heroics and bellicose self-justification (to reappear, alas, only too soon) these few quiet moments of universal compassion are a refreshment and a rest.

Britain's *Frieda* (1947, Basil Dearden), though somewhat slight and stagey, deals intelligently with a contemporary problem—the acceptance by an English family of a German girl whom an RAF officer has married to save her from the consequences of having helped him to escape from P-O-W camp.

The finest film of the time, however, indeed among the finest of all time, was Carol Reed's *The Third Man* (1949). The basic plot—the search for and eventual death of a black market racketeer in postwar Vienna—matters little, gripping though it is as a thriller;

it is the atmosphere that makes this picture the masterpiece it is. The weary, cold aftermath of a devastating defeat permeates every scene: the battered city itself, with its gimcrack offices and tawdry, shabby homes in the midst of ruined ornate buildings, is both a background to and a symbol of the human existence dragged out within it—of the whole grotesque muddle into which we have all allowed ourselves to fall. The film loses not a jot of its power over the years. However many times it is seen, it haunts the mind anew with its picture of a town, a generation, a world in defeat. Much of this is due to the performances that Reed has drawn from his superb cast—particularly Alida Valli, but most of all Trevor Howard brilliantly portraying a man doing a dull, distasteful job without illusions, with little hope, but as best he may. To pick on any one aspect of *The Third Man* is to be unfair to the rest—to Carol Reed's all-round direction, to Graham Greene's script, to the famous zither music of Anton Karas, the photography of Robert Krasker, the art direction of Vincent Korda, the editing of Oswald Hafenrichter. Rarely can the atmosphere, the feel, the sound, the look, the very smell of a postwar existence in

Trevor Howard, Joseph Cotten and Bernard Lee in Carol Reed's masterpiece, THE THIRD MAN.

a beaten city have been captured with such piercing accuracy as in this masterpiece of the cinema. It closes on the famous shot of Harry Lime's girl walking down the long leaf-strewn avenue, approaching—and passing—the waiting Holly Martins. It is a shot perfectly calculated in mood and tempo, and one is hearteningly aware of having been given, for the past ninety minutes, an all too rare glimpse of what great film-making can achieve.

The respite was short. Already by 1948 "war dramas" were reappearing, the start of a flood that was to swamp the cinema almost without let-up for twenty years. *Jungle Patrol* (Joe Newman), *Fighter Squadron* (Raoul Walsh), *Command Decision* (Sam Wood)—the titles alone of this 1948 bunch were warning of what was to come. In 1949 appeared *Battleground* (William Wellman), dedicated to "the battered bastards of Bastogne" (and also, presumably, to making money), reconstructing part of the Battle of the Bulge; and *The Sands of Iwo Jima* (Allan Dwan)—John Wayne hammering away at his men, who naturally grow to love him by the final fade-out, and also at the Japs, who kill him—temporarily. In *The Halls of Montezuma* (1950) Lewis Milestone finally threw off the tattered shreds of the man who made *All Quiet on the Western Front* and sallied against the designated foe (Japs) with a wild cinematic scream.

Of more worth is Henry King's *Twelve O'Clock High* (1949) a slow but penetrating study of how a commander, brought in to boost the morale of an Air Force group that has been "growing soft" under a kindly chief, is able to do so only at the cost of his own mental, physical and spiritual health. It is, intentional or not, a caustic comment on the essential vileness of the war mentality, whatever "purpose" is put forward for its nourishment. The film is notable also for a magnificent performance from Gregory Peck as the haunted officer.

Britain brought forth *Morning Departure* (1949, Roy Baker), a sincere if not unusual story of men trapped in a submarine sunk by a floating mine; *They Were Not Divided* (1950, Terence Young), a drearily superficial story of the period leading up to the Normandy invasion; and the first of the hearty p-o-w escape films, *The Wooden Horse* (1950, Jack Lee). There is an apparently inevitable sort of public school atmosphere about nearly all these escape pictures even when, as in this case, they are founded on fact. It seems a disservice to the thousands who endured years of degrading and spirit-eroding detention to emphasise to such an extent the image of the schoolboy breaking bounds.

From Britain, too, came the first of the new crop of awful-warning films—the tense and gripping *Seven Days to Noon* (1950, John Boult-

Professor on the run: Barry Jones in SEVEN DAYS TO NOON.

ing), in which a scientist working on atomic research is suddenly stricken by conscience (and therefore considered to be mad), and threatens to blow up London unless work on the Bomb is stopped. Needless to say, he is prevented, and we can all heave a sigh of relief that the production of even bigger and better bombs can now safely proceed. Joseph Losey's *The Boy with Green Hair* (1948) is an anti-war allegory that unfortunately becomes rather lost in its fairytale element. All the same, it contrives to make a few pertinent comments on the apparent death-wish of a sizable section of the human race.

Two memorable postwar productions from Germany were *The Murderers Are among Us* (*Die Mörder sind unter uns,* 1947, Wolfgang Staudte) and *Germany Year Zero* (*Germania anno zero,* 1948), a Franco/German undertaking directed by the Italian Roberto Rossellini. Both paint grim pictures of life in a shattered land—stories unfolding in surroundings of ruin and desolation. The misery of life in the broken city is nowhere minimised, yet the lack of self-pity is surprisingly absent. It is interesting to view these two films in the light of the rebuilt Germany of today.

Finally, before plunging into the murky waters of the Fifties,

84

Confrontation: the children in Joseph Losey's THE BOY WITH GREEN HAIR.

brief mention must be made of Alain Resnais's *Guernica* (1950). During the course of eleven minutes, taking Picasso's famous fresco as his starting point and using as text Paul Eluard's poem on the infamous bombing assault, the director paints his own individually styled picture of the full horror of destruction, as exemplified in what happened to one small village in Spain.

Jim Brown in action in THE DIRTY DOZEN.

7. Korea to Kwai

OF ALL THE WAR FILMS that have yet appeared those of the Korean fighting, taken as a whole, make the most dismal viewing. *Korea Patrol* (1951, Max Nosseck), *Steel Helmet* and *The Fixed Bayonet* (both 1951, Samuel Fuller), *Battle Zone* (1952, Lesley Selander), *One Minute to Zero* (1952, Tay Garnett), *Retreat, Hell!* (1952, Joseph Lewis), *Cease Fire* (1953, Owen Crump), which even "amazing 3-D" could not save, *Prisoner of War* (1954, Andrew Marton)—title after title follow in a gruesome procession of screaming hatred, glorified violence and dim mediocrity. *The Glory Brigade* (1953, Robert D. Webb) and *The Bridges at Toko-Ri* (1954, Mark Robson) each make some attempt to rise above the general crudity, but look good only by comparison with the rest. Two later films, *Battle Hymn* (1956, Douglas Sirk) and *Men in War* (1957, Anthony Mann) consider to a certain extent the moral aspects of the campaign, but apart from these doubtful exceptions it is difficult to think of a single picture worth the celluloid it is printed on. Presumably they had the required effect on those for whom they were primarily intended, but viewed dispassionately they give rise to an uncomfortable feeling that anyone protesting so much must be somewhat doubtful as to the justice of their cause—surely an unintended reaction.

Meanwhile Second World War productions began to proliferate anew—with, here and there, significant changes of attitude and emphasis. A new enemy has been found—perhaps, therefore, the old one was not so bad after all. In *The Desert Fox* (*Rommel—Desert Fox*, 1951, Henry Hathaway) the German commander (predictably "anti-Nazi") is represented in so sympathetic a light—played by the excellent and popular James Mason—that the film was not altogether favourably received in certain quarters. The balance had to be redressed in *Desert Rats* (1953, Robert Wise), about the siege of Tobruk. In *The Sea Chase* (1955, John Farrow), a thriller set in the

James Mason as ROMMEL—DESERT FOX.

early years of the war, the part of a German sea-captain ("anti-Nazi" again) is played by none other than that redoubtable American pillar John Wayne.

During the same period old-time Second World War films continued to appear. From the European front came *Force of Arms* (1951, Michael Curtiz) an attempt at the Hemingway tough-sentimental; *Target Unknown* (1951, George Sherman); *Decision before Dawn* (1951, Anatole Litvak); *Stalag 17* (1953, Billy Wilder), fun and games with pompous Nazis in a prison camp; and *D-Day the Sixth of June* (1956, Henry Koster), the Normandy invasion seen as a means of settling the tangled love life of Lt. Col. Wynter, Capt. Brad Parker, and little Nurse Valerie. From the Japanese theatre of war the cinemagoer had the choice of *Flying Leathernecks* (1951, Nicholas Ray), a paean to violence almost equalling the Korean product at its worst; *Okinawa* (1952, Leigh Jason); *Thunder across the Pacific* (1952, Allan Dwan), and others of the same sort. Among the best of the bunch were *Eight Iron Men* (1952, Edward Dmytryk), *The Caine Mutiny* (1954, also from Edward Dmyrtyk) and *Attack!* (1956, Robert Aldrich). *The Caine Mutiny,* best known of the three, is dominated by Humphrey Bogart's fine performance as the neurotic Captain Queeg, and is at its best in the tense court-martial scene, but is weakened by a shallow, fairy-tale (and probably obligatory) ending.

Attack!, though showing signs of the delight in brutality and the nihilistic cynicism that were to lead the director on the downward path to *The Dirty Dozen* (1967) , at least demonstrates that inefficiency, corruption and cowardice may be found on both sides in any conflict. It is at base, however, a defeatist, and indeed pernicious film, attacking not war but only the incompetent waging of it. *Eight Iron Men,* an adaptation of a play by Harry Brown, author of *A Walk in the Sun,* deals with the reactions of a group of soldiers refused permission to risk their lives to rescue another who is trapped in a shell-hole. It is taut, exciting and commendably restrained, with a nicely ironical conclusion to its fairly unoriginal situation.

From Here to Eternity (1953, Fred Zinnemann), though only marginally concerned with the subject of war, presents what is probably as clear a picture as any of the chaos following the attack on Pearl Harbor.

Altogether, viewing American war films of the period, one is left with the impression that those responsible were uncertain which way to face—apart from towards the box-office.

In a smaller way Britain, too, was fully aware of the profit potential in the subject, though the tone was generally less hysterical. Films such as *Angels One Five* (1952, George More O'Ferrall) , *The*

Chaos after the bomb in ANGELS ONE FIVE.

Red Beret (1953, Terence Young), *Albert RN* (1953, Lewis Gilbert), *Above Us the Waves* (1955, Ralph Thomas), *Cockleshell Heroes* (1955, José Ferrer) are unremarkable adventure stories of variable competence, concerned with the Navy, Air Force, parachute troops, prison camps, etc., etc.▪*The Cruel Sea*▪(1953, Charles Frend, from Nicholas Monsarrat's lengthy best-seller) is a rather more ambitious undertaking, with a look at the Battle of the Atlantic that is astringent, realistic and grim. *Malta Story* (1953, Brian Desmond Hurst) was released as a tribute to the tenacious islanders, but proved to be more story than Malta. Similarly *The Colditz Story* (1954, Guy Hamilton) —forerunner of an apparently interminable television series—treats the whole business of wartime imprisonment once again as a schoolboy lark—somewhat unpleasant at times, but awfully thrilling if you can work out an escape plan.

The great success of *The Dam Busters* (1955, Michael Anderson) must shoulder the grave responsibility of increasing the flow of war films still further. In itself it is an able reconstruction of a violently destructive project. The immense and ingenious models appear as such, but compel admiration for the skill of their builders. Towards

Model work for THE DAM BUSTERS.

90

the close of the film there is a brief moment of moral stock-taking, when the loss of life involved is weighed against the success of the mission: of British life, that is—the fate of any unfortunate farmers or families whose homes were in the path of the loosened floodwaters is less closely considered. *A Town Like Alice* (1956, Jack Lee), one of the few British features set in Malaya, showed national *sang-froid* reduced almost to freezing point, no single member of the party of civilians caught in the hands of the Japanese cracking by so much as a millimetre. The film contained much atmosphere, however, and an intelligent if low-keyed script. *Reach for the Sky* (1956, Lewis Gilbert), the story of Douglas Bader, rather unhappily qualifies for the adjective "worthy." It is a saga of one man's courage in overcoming fearful odds (the loss of both legs in a flying accident), with interpolated action sequences. With such a theme even a poorly made film could scarcely fail to be effective, and *Reach for the Sky* is both competent and honest. Nevertheless, the fact that the subject of a true story is still very much a living legend—a "war hero" portrayed by a popular star (Kenneth More)—unavoidably results in a sense of restraint, of discreet manipulation, of hands to some extent tied.

The Battle of the River Plate (*Pursuit of the Graf Spee*, 1956, Michael Powell and Emeric Pressburger) is a conscientious, scrupulously fair, and—alas—rather flat reconstruction of the famous naval engagement that resulted in the sinking of the "Graf Spee." It has none of the panache, the refreshing disregard of the canons of "good taste" or the exhilarating flamboyance of other Powell and Pressburger productions. The cool eye of truth is again a restraining factor.

*   *   *

The most impressive foreign language films of the time were the Polish trilogy. *A Generation* (*Pokolenie*, 1954). *Kanał* (1956) and *Ashes and Diamonds* (*Popiół i diament*, 1958), directed by Andrzej Wajda. The first traces the growth and training of a young man and his friends from hooligans into fervent partisan fighters; the second recounts the adventures and tragic end of a group of partisans during the Warsaw Uprising who are driven to take refuge in the city sewers; the action of the third takes place immediately after the German surrender, under the grim threat of civil war. Over and above the personal stories they tell, all three are patterns of the political situations of the time, shot through with bitter anger and despair. They seem to picture a haunted country's attempt to exorcise its memories of terror and tragedy. None is a masterpiece, all are too enclosed in

From Wajda's Polish trilogy: above—KANAL; below—ASHES AND DIA-MONDS.

private and personal worlds to have more than a limited significance in time or place. As human documents, however, all three—and particularly the most intimate, *Kanał*—are of lasting interest.

From Russia came only vast reconstructions: *The Battle of Stalingrad* (*Stalingradskaya bitva,* in two parts, 1950, Vladimir Petrov), *The Fall of Berlin* (*Padyeniye Berlina,* 1950, Mikhail Chiaureli). The latter caricatures her allies as fiercely as her enemies. None has much interest save as spectacle, and as an example of how to angle history.

Among the few striking productions were two from former foes, Germany and Japan. *Wozzeck* (Georg Klaren), made in 1947 but not shown publicly in Britain until 1953 and then only in a mutilated version, is an updating of Georg Buchner's famous 140-year-old play, a violent attack on Prussian militarism and discipline, stylised to free it from temporal confines. It is almost a return to the films made in Germany just after the First World War, and might be regarded as a nation's revulsion (after suffering a military defeat) from militarism. Japan's *The Burmese Harp* (*Biruma no Tategoto,* 1956, Kon Ichi-

Kurt Meisel as WOZZECK.

Above—Soldier into monk; below—Soldiers' Chorus: two scenes from the Japanese masterpiece, THE BURMESE HARP.

kawa), though also presented in a stylised form, has nothing in common with the film of its former ally. A young Japanese soldier in Burma, nursed back from near-death by a Buddhist monk, chooses, when the war is over, to join the order himself and to remain in Burma, where earlier he had honoured the scattered unburied dead with burial. The picture is a poetic lament for a defeated world, and a qualified message of hope for an uncertain future. In 1959 Kon Ichikawa directed *Fires on the Plain* (*Nobi*), equally strong and compassionate in theme and treatment as it follows the appalling sufferings of a tubercular young private during the closing days of the war.

From France came René Clément's great *Les jeux interdits* (1952), dealing in the main with the effect of adult example on child behaviour, but opening with truly terrifying shots of a brief attack by German planes on a column of refugees, and closing with a tragic glimpse of the small lost child whose parents were killed and who,

Little girl lost—a tragedy of war from René Clément's subtle and moving film LES JEUX INTERDITS.

after having briefly found a strange haven, is once more deprived of both her family and the boy who befriended her—war and religious bigotry equally to blame.

*   *   *

Of other wars, the Crimean made a rare appearance with William Castle's *Charge of the Lancers* (U.S., 1953), a singularly pointless effort about the delivery of a new gun for use against the Russians at Sebastopol; and Napoléon in the handsomely mounted *War and Peace* (1956), King Vidor), in which the director joined forces with scriptwriters Bridget Boland, Robert Westerby, Mario Camerini, Ennio De Concini and Ivo Perilli to encompass the effective subversion of the significance of Tolstoy's work. They were helped by the incomprehensible miscasting of the fine actor Henry Fonda as Pierre.

The American Civil War fared a little better. *The Raid* (1954, Hugo Fregonese) and *Escape from Fort Bravo* (1953, John Sturges) are conventional action pieces; and *The Great Locomotive Chase* (1956, Francis D. Lyon) has no pretensions to be more than the "true version"—told to the children—of Buster Keaton's *The General*. *The Red Badge of Courage* (1951, John Huston), however, is a near—if

Audie Murphy, left foreground, in THE RED BADGE OF COURAGE.

96

flawed—masterpiece. The story of the alleged murder of the film by the producers is well-known and, though finally issued for consideration as a complete work, it cannot fairly be judged except as a mutilated one. What are left are some well staged battle scenes (impossible to avoid reference to Brady's photographs), and a very superficial study of a coward's "regeneration." It may well be that we have the best of the film in the fine action sequences. Audie Murphy, "most decorated soldier of the Second World War," here earns no medals as an actor—and considerable acting ability would be necessary to make Stephen Crane's fairly tall story believable in the cold light of the projector's beam.

Best of all Civil War films, and arguably best of a whole depressing period, is *A Time out of War* (1954, direction and script by Denis Sanders from a story by Robert W. Chambers). Three soldiers—two Northerners, one Southerner—on picket duty on either side of a river, agree to observe their own brief truce. They chat, rest, float coffee and tobacco to one another across the river. The discovery of the body of a dead soldier brings them sharply back to reality. They bury him, fire a salute together in his honour, then return to their business of death. In the brief twenty-three minutes of this visually beautiful little masterpiece more is said on its subject than in a dozen overblown epics.

Finally, though in general there is not the space available to include the animated film, mention must be made of Norman McLaren's biting little allegory *Neighbors* (1952). Two men are sitting in deck chairs on either side of their garden boundary. A flower grows up exactly between them, and they start to quarrel over it, growing progressively more violent, until finally they destroy everything and everybody, including themselves. In the midst of the ruin and destruction the flower reappears. By ingenious camera work the two men move in little jerks like puppets. This accentuates their automatism, and paradoxically at one and the same time appears both to increase and decrease their "human-ness." The mannikin figures are combined with drawings in a trenchant comment on the total imbecility of war.

At the end of the period under review, as the murky flood of Korean pictures dwindled to a trickle, there appeared on the warfilm horizon the vanguard of what might be called the neo-epic army— led by *The Bridge on the River Kwai*.

*THE BRIDGE ON THE RIVER KWAI: above—the bridge completed;
below—the destroyers, Jack Hawkins and William Holden.*

8. Era of Epics

WITH THE COMING of the late Fifties there arrived the age of the War Epic, which coincided more or less closely with the decline of the big studios, the growth of the independents, and the blurring of national film boundaries. For the next dozen years or so these huge, lumbering, blunt-edged productions were, "like wounded snakes," to drag their slow lengths along the wide screen. Often multi-national and multi-lingual, the name of the director (or directors) merely one in a long list of technical credits, they seemed to have little to offer except spectacle, little to say except "look how big I am." Any personal style or statement was swamped by the vastness and complexity of the whole undertaking. With few exceptions they were essentially anonymous commercial mass products, their primary purpose, one can only conclude, to make money, since facts were so often distorted to suit fiction. They did not even propagate propaganda—at least to any extent—because efforts not to offend (and thereby lose bookings in) any country were so obviously of prime importance. Announcements of "a tribute" to this, that or the other could not but be accepted with a certain reserve when it was noted how abruptly production dwindled when they failed to be profitable.

David Lean's *The Bridge on the River Kwai* (1957) may fairly claim to be both the first and the best of this particular school of mammoths. It is also the most personal. The bridge, an important link in Japanese communications, is being built—and sabotaged—by prisoners-of-war. After a confrontation with the Japanese commandant, the newly arrived Colonel Nicholson determines that all this shall be altered—that the bridge shall instead be constructed as close to perfection as possible, that it shall be a monument to British efficiency and invincibility. Meanwhile, unkown to him, a small commando force is sent out to destroy it. In a confused climactic struggle Nicholson and others are killed. As he falls dead, the Colonel falls on a detonator, triggering off explosives set to destroy the bridge. Apart from its totally riveting suspense story the film is an essay in irony which each viewer will interpret in his own way according to where his sympathies lie. The confusion and uncertainty of the final moments are thus seen to be deliberate: the doctor's cry of "Madness, madness!" will mean whatever the viewer, with his particular prejudices, considers it ought to mean. The film had a notable and deserved success, and made a considerable stir in the muddy waters of the contemporary war film.

Dunkirk (1958, Leslie Norman), has been described by Sir Michael Balcon as perhaps the largest-scale picture with which he had ever been connected—a spectacular reconstruction built round the experiences of one small group of men. The subject—one of the inspiring moments in the generally less than inspiring history of nations

John Mills in DUNKIRK.

—is almost infallible, and generally this film, though dealing with conventional types in conventional manner, does not fail.

The Guns of Navarone (1961, J. Lee Thompson), dealing with the destruction of two monster German guns by a small detail of men on the island of Kheros, is really not much more than a modest-scale war adventure blown up to epic size. Carl Foreman, who both produced and wrote the script from Alistair MacLean's book, was later to make a far more personal statement in *The Victors* (1963): here, any still small voice is lost in the general din of action.

In 1962 dawned *The Longest Day*, which unhappily at moments felt like The Longest Film. It was graced with four directors (Ken Annakin, Andrew Marton, Bernhard Wicki and Darryl F. Zanuck), one battle-scene co-ordinator, four assistant directors and five script-writers. The fact that it holds together as well as it does is presumably due to the skill of the single editor, Samuel E. Beetley. Covering the final preparations for, the launching of, and the immediate aftermath of the Normandy invasion, it is based on Cornelius Ryan's book of ingeniously dovetailed reminiscences, and contains the usual array of familiar star faces to weaken authenticity; it is, like so many block-busters, temporarily impressive and thereafter impossible to remember except as a vague blur of guns, swirling seas, falling buildings,

John Wayne, familiarly controlled and controlling in THE LONGEST DAY. Robert Ryan on the right.

boats, lanes, smoke and soldiers, soldiers running, jumping and standing still. It is, essentially, a tennis net of a film—void spaces joined together by strings of anecdotes.

The Great Escape (1962, John Sturges) is a U.S./West Germany collaboration—prisoners-of-war on a large scale, details familiar. The niceties of tunnel-digging are interesting, if much the same as hitherto, and the underground atmosphere—sportive if a trifle grim—cheerfully maintained. That said, little remains.

Carl Foreman's one-man-band, *The Victors* (1963, he wrote, pro-

A shattered Jeanne Moreau in THE VICTORS.

duced and directed), has not had a wholly favourable reception, being accused of turgidity and over-emphasis. At least, though, it bears the stamp of a personality and utters an indivdual statement—that, in a 175-minute star-studded "epic," is something of an achievement in itself. It is a fervent attack on every aspect and result of waging war, slammed home with an energy that, if at moments is slightly exasperating, at least leaves no doubt of the slammer's sincerity. The film calls for inclusion here for its widely embracing approach to its subject rather than its size: apart from length it is not on a particularly large scale. Foreman has said that he felt the need for "a completely personal statement based on complete responsibility," and one may admit that he has made it.

In Harm's Way (1965, Otto Preminger) says in 167 minutes what is scarcely worth saying in eighty—that John Wayne may lose an early battle, but is sure to win in the end. It also appears to say, perhaps less intentionally, that naval officers and the women with whom they associate are, almost without exception, either unpleasant or uninteresting. This, one feels confident, is far from the truth, but the reason for making it appear true on film is difficult to fathom. In

John Wayne and Tom Tryon IN HARM'S WAY.

1965 Great Britain joined with Italy to produce *Operation Crossbow* (Michael Anderson) a large and not uninteresting picture about the destruction of the V-weapon installations at Peenemunde. Characters (fictional) are cardboard and the story is trite. But the background appears reasonably authentic, and one feels that in this respect at least this is a film of some value as big screen reportage. Equally this is true of *The Train* (1964, John Frankenheimer), one of the better of its kind and one whose length does not seem unduly stretched. This multi-national film (U.S./France/Italy) suffers from the usual inept dubbing, but it tells an exciting story (an attempt by the French Resistance to prevent valuable works of art from being moved to Germany in 1944), and tells it well. Paul Scofield is allowed to present an altogether credible, if demon-possessed, German officer, and Frankenheimer proves again what has been proved before, that the steam train can outdo any star, dog, cat or child in glamour. The film makes a pertinent, if not very original, comment about the differing values set on objects (whether *objets d'art* or not) and human beings. Sidney

Photogenic rolling stock in Frankenheimer's THE TRAIN.

Burt Lancaster faces Paul Scofield in THE TRAIN.

Lumet's remarkable *The Hill* (1965) also has an object as a leading character, but of a very different kind. It concerns the treatment of a handful of prisoners sent to a military detention camp during the North African campaign, where they are made to climb up and down an artificial hill while carrying full equipment. The story eventually blows up into frenetic melodrama, but the earlier part—grittily photographed by Oswald Morris—is a remarkable study of sustained tension and smouldering resentment, with bravura performances from Harry Andrews and Ian Hendry as the tormentors.

A contemporary critic remarked of *The Battle of the Bulge* (1965, Ken Annakin) that it probably did not resemble the Ardennes offensive at all, but this did not matter because it was such an exciting war story. This is, to put it mildly, a strange view to take. A film calling itself *The Battle of the Bulge,* deliberately playing down on "characterisation" and up on details of tank battles and sieges, is accurate (or as accurate as possible) or it is nothing. Without some value as "historical reconstruction" it has nothing whatever to offer,

'Accurate or nothing': a scene from THE BATTLE OF THE BULGE.

apart from the contrived suspense of a clockwork thriller—on an "epic" scale, naturally.

René Clément's *Is Paris Burning?* (*Paris, brûle-t-il?*, 1965) is a sad disappointment after his wonderful "fringe" war film *Les jeux interdits*. It is, in fact, an untidy, anti-climactic muddle, dealing with the liberation of the French capital in August 1944, beginning with the grave disadvantage that we already know the answer to the famous question.

Two more large-scale works appeared towards the end of the decade: from America *The Bridge at Remagen* (1968, John Guillermin); from Britain *Battle of Britain* (1969, Guy Hamilton). Both are earnestly fair to both sides, but the former (dealing with the crossing of the Rhine bridge, but without tying itself down too much to dull truth) at least has a certain sardonic bite. *Battle of Britain* is a large, bland, worthy, expensive, star-studded "tribute," with all that somewhat forbidding word implies. The air battles are efficiently done—though one face in a cockpit confusingly resembles any other— and the noise of explosions and general destruction is all very stimulating. Once again, however, there is a hollow centre, an essential nothingness. Does a "tribute" have to say so little besides? Even as

A striking air combat still from BATTLE OF BRITAIN.

spectacle *Battle of Britain* is only spasmodically convincing; the blitz, in particular, still fails to yield up its atmosphere. Only the figure of Laurence Olivier's lonely, stubborn, forbidding yet somehow pathetic Dowding remains in the memory for much longer than it takes to leave the theatre. The rest is a blurred image of all the other air films that ever were. More seriously, no sense of the importance of those days and nights comes across—instead we are treated to routine comedy and trivial personalities. Epic films, it seems, are not adequate to celebrate epic events.

*   *   *

Turning from blockbusters to the general run of war films during the late Fifties and the Sixties, one is appalled above all at their sheer proliferation. There is something more than a shade unpalatable in

Spectacular destruction in 633 SQUADRON.

Two fine performances in an equally fine film: Leslie French and Paul Massie in ORDERS TO KILL.

108

the picture of every little film man digging for little nuggets in the most appalling and tragic landslide in the world's history. Some a little better than average, some a little worse, one after another they rolled off the spools. From America came *The Naked and the Dead* (1958, Raoul Walsh), *When Hell Broke Loose* (1957, Kenneth Crane), *The Young Lions* (1958, Edward Dmytryk, with a blond Marlon Brando), *The Battle of the Coral Sea* (1959, Paul Wendkos), *The Battle on the Beach* (1961, Herbert Coleman), *Merrill's Marauders* (1962, Samuel Fuller), *Shell Shock* (1963, J. P. Hayes), *Back Door to Hell* (1964, Monte Hellman), *The 1000 Plane Raid* (1968, Boris Sagal); from Britain, *Battle of the V1* (1958, Vernon Sewell), *The Camp on Blood Island* (1958, Val Guest), *Tarnished Heroes* (1961, Ernest Morris), *Foxhole in Cairo* (1960, John Moxey), *Mystery Submarine* (1963, C. M. Pennington-Richards), *633 Squadron* (1964, Walter Grauman), *Play Dirty* (1968, André de Toth). Singly these films are insignificant, but taken together they add up to a formidable amount of forgettable screen time, a record of unoriginal and profitless (except at the box office) retrospection.

More pernicious than such dull stuff is the type of film exemplified in the joint U.S./British production *The Dirty Dozen,* (1967, Robert Aldrich) with its glorification of violence nastily concealed under a shiny cloak of sentimentality. The "dozen"—convicted criminals of a particularly loathsome type—finish as heroes who sacrifice their lives. The one point that such a film makes, intentionally or not, is the truth of the saying that in war the scum is brought to the surface: it seems that this applies to the cinema also.

The comparatively few Korean films of these years—*Hell Is for Heroes* (1962, Don Siegel), *Marines, Let's Go* (1961, Raoul Walsh), *War Hero* (1960, Burt Topper), *The Nun and the Sergeant* (1962, Franklin Adreon), etc.—remain mostly at the abysmal level of earlier periods. An exception is *War Hunt* (1961, Denis Sanders), which courageously and uncompromisingly speaks out about the evil influence of the war mentality, and by implication against the type of film that obliquely or directly fosters it.

It is a relief to turn to the handful of more worthwhile films dealing with the two World Wars that appeared during this melancholy period, nearly all of them from Britain. *Orders to Kill* (1958, Anthony Asquith) is for most of its length a powerful indictment, concerning an American bomber pilot sent to occupied Paris in 1944 to kill an allied agent suspected of treachery. Brought face to face with the necessity of killing at close quarters instead of anonymously from a distance, he is brought also to a horrifying realisation of just what such an act means. Unfortunately the impact is weakened towards the film's close, when a glib officer comforts the distraught young man with patriotic platitudes—in wartime conscience may, or must, be honourably ignored. If these scenes are meant as satire, this is too subtle to be perceptible.

Reach for Glory (1961, Philip Leacock) on the other hand, pulls no punches at all. Under Leacock's outstandingly sensitive direction this brilliant small-scale film, telling of the effects of war conditions and military propaganda on a group of young boys evacuated to a somewhat boring "safe area," extends far beyond its immediate circumstances to become a universally valid accusation and warning. It should be compulsorily prescribed as an antidote to every bellicose blockbuster. Equally uncompromising is Joseph Losey's *King and Country* (1964), about the execution of a private soldier for desertion during the First World War, and showing how a group of mainly

Tom Courtenay and Dirk Bogarde, equally superb in KING AND COUN-TRY.

110

kindly and decent men can be caught in a trap like the rats that over-run the trenches, and find themselves able to consent to and partici-pate in a cruel and filthy procedure because the rules of war enable them to shelve their personal responsibility. The soldier, it is inter-esting to note, is not a conscript but a volunteer who was urged to join by women at home. Had he lost his limbs or his sight he would have been acclaimed an honourable war victim; because he loses his nerve, he is shot. These three films are outstanding among all from either Britain or America during the early and middle Sixties.

Lawrence of Arabia (1962, David Lean) does not claim to be a strict historical record of either the Palestinian campaign of the First World War or of the life of its hero, and should not therefore be judged as such. As spectacle it is magnificent; as an example of dis-creet whitewashing and myth preservation it is ingenious; as a picture of Arab train wrecking and horse riding it is exciting. Beyond this it is mute.

At the other end of the scale of size, *It Happened Here* (1963),

Peter O'Toole as a somewhat glamorised LAWRENCE OF ARABIA.

Kevin Brownlow's and Andrew Mollo's shoe-string production, started when they were in their 'teens and adhered to, with incredible tenacity, for over seven years, is an ingenious and imaginative picture of what it might have been like in Britain if Hitler had successfully invaded the country. An anti-Nazi rather than anti-war film, it re-creates the surface atmosphere of the drab days with an accuracy particularly impressive from two young film-makers who were about three years of age at the time, and then proceeds to paint a chilling picture of

England under the Nazis: IT HAPPENED HERE.

"ourselves" which "we" might glance at before being too ready to condemn others to whom the situation was only too real.

Guns at Batasi (1964, John Guillermin) is not a war film in the true sense, but a rather touching tribute to the simple-minded, brazen-voiced, wooden-headed, noble-spirited RSM (wonderfully portrayed by Richard Attenborough)—reminding us that there is a great deal to be said for the soldierly virtues (particularly when contrasted with the devious shiftings of the political mind), but demonstrating at the

Richard Attenborough's excellent characterization in GUNS AT BATASI.

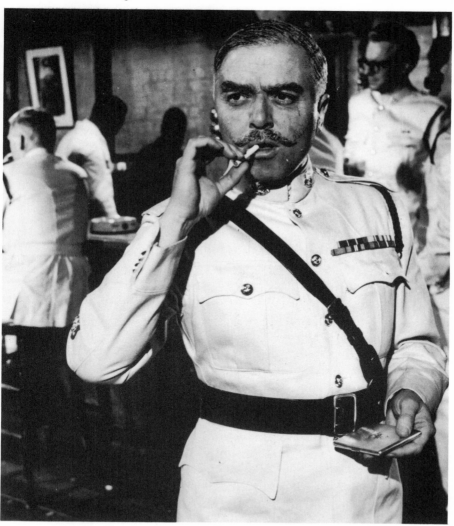

same time that bravery and single-minded loyalty can, if allied to stupidity, be the greatest danger of all. The film, set in a state in the African Commonwealth that had recently acquired independence, is notable for some magnificent black-and-white photography on the wide screen by Douglas Slocombe.

King Rat (1965) is an American production directed by the Englishman Bryan Forbes and with a mainly British cast. It manages to vary the threadbare P-O-W formula, dealing with the lives of the men inside their camp rather than with the usual escape attempts, and demonstrating that frustration and boredom do not necessarily make heroes, however noble the cause. Bryan Forbes works up an uncompromising and oddly sinister atmosphere of petty tyranny and corruption, only occasionally losing the threads and slackening the tension among the crowd of characters. Peter Collinson's *The Long Day's Dying* (1968), contrasts the cool mechanics of killing with the ghastly realities of dying, in a tightly knit story of three lost paratroopers and their German prisoner attempting to find their way back to their own unit. The men, wandering in a vast, impersonal, menacing landscape, are representative of men so trapped in any place, at any time, in any war, and this very anonymity gives the story a wider relevance. The film, admittedly overstated in places, has several sequences of very considerable power. It certainly did not deserve to become, as it appears to have become, one of the many "lost films" in this incomprehensible industry.

The very entertaining *Where Eagles Dare* (1968, Brian G. Hutton) is one of the few genuine war-film send-ups apart from the knockout comedy and the anti-war satire. The story of a group of men rescuing a captured officer from the Nazis high in the Alps—and splendidly led by Richard Burton—is told with cunningly exaggerated heroics (from a script by Alistair MacLean based on his own novel), so that it is only gradually that we realise what is happening. The realisation is refreshing. Even heroism is all the better for an occasional laugh at itself.

Returning to the First World War we encounter *The Blue Max* (1966, John Guillermin), an aerial epic about an ambitious German air ace. It has not much more, or less, to offer than similar aerial epics past and to come. The reproductions of the 1918 landscapes, and in particular of the planes, are magnificent, Douglas Slocombe's photography is as good as anything he has done—which is saying a great deal—and the sky battles (directed by Tony Squire) are exciting. It is obvious that no (or not much) expense has been spared, and everything is very efficiently done. When that has been said, though, there

Two grim scenes from Peter Collinson's too-rarely screened THE LONG DAY'S DYING.

Dealing with an attack on an airfield in the First World War: THE BLUE MAX.

is nothing else to add. Once again there is the essentially trivial use of a world tragedy as background. Everyone knows by now that aeroplanes (1918 or 1944) look fine swooping in the sky, and when there is so little of substance besides (except Ursula Andress) it hardly seems worth the trouble.

Of more interest, though no epic, is Stephen Weeks's *1917* (1968), a little-seen, cheaply budgeted, well-photographed short about an incident that occurred between two closely opposing trenches—made without spectacle, without stars, but with distinction. *Oh! What a Lovely War* (1969), Richard Attenborough's first venture as director, is based on a stage production (by Joan Littlewood's "Theatre Workshop") which in its turn derived from a radio feature by Charles Chilton entitled "The Long Long Trail." It is a re-creation, rather than a transference, and is wholly successful. The film succeeds in its blasting attack primarily by revealing the bitterness and futile tragedy underlying what are often presented nowadays as cosily nostalgic music-hall songs. The well-known use of Brighton Pier, with its peepshows, slot machines, miniature railway and pavilion, to represent scenes at home and elsewhere is a brilliant *tour de force*—reaching its

116

The statesmen—on Brighton Pier: from OH! WHAT A LOVELY WAR.

highest point, literally as well as metaphorically, in the ivory tower helter-skelter on which stand the top brass as they play their little soldier games with human lives. The changes to and from the artificiality of the sea resort to the reality of the trench scenes and other naturalistic settings are contrived without any jarring inconsistency by the cunning use of the peepshow machines. Highly ingenious, too, is the employment of instantly recognisable screen stars to play the rulers, generals and politicians, in contrast to the mainly anonymous Smith family and the deliberately unmemorable figures dying in shell-holes. Another astonishingly successful inspiration is the beach photographer (played with a wonderfully controlled hint of the sinister by Joe Melia) who serves in the early part of the film as a link between the events on-screen and the audience, and later merges more into the background to take a mysterious hand in the manipulation of those events as if from a shadowy Olympus. A measure of the film's success is that it never falls into the trap of its own songs—never becomes an easy shedding of tears over old, unhappy, far-off things. Though its impact is obviously of a different kind on the dwindling numbers of those who may have actually lived through the 1914–18 years, it speaks to the world of today with equal cogency. It also serves as a reminder to the emotionally immature of any age who scorn the sacri-

117

The lighter side: a scene of dalliance from WHAT DID YOU DO IN THE WAR, DADDY?

fices and sufferings of past generations, that their own attitudes, actions and sacrifices may well prove as futile and foolish to those who reap the benefits—if any. *Oh! What a Lovely War* is a memorial and a summing up, and the famous panoramic closing shot of massed symbolic graves is among the most poignant and eloquent moments in the cinema.

In the documentary field, *Blitz on Britain* (1960) is a useful, if

118

not particularly inspiring, record of the twelve months from May 10, 1940 to the last big raid on London in May 1941, gathered from German and British newsreels and documentaries by Harry Booth, and accompanied by Alistair Cooke as commentator. It smacks a little of the typical television compilation, but at least it is an antidote to the falsity of the fictional representations of its subject, and its brevity (ten minutes) compels it to present a coherent account of a time that needs no trumpets to underscore its tragedy and its fortitude.

*   *   *

Apart from the titles already mentioned, neither in quality nor quantity did America have as much to say about the two World Wars during the period under scrutiny. The singularly pointless updating of *The Four Horsemen of the Apocalypse* (1961, Vincente Minnelli) is best quickly buried. More interesting is Roger Corman's *The Secret Invasion* (1964), showing how the theme of utilising the skill of the criminal to "better" purpose in war can be treated to make a significant statement, in contrast to the dumb, coarse crudities of *The Dirty Dozen. What Did You Do in the War, Daddy?* (1966, Blake Edwards)

How to enjoy your war: James Coburn in WHAT DID YOU DO IN THE WAR, DADDY?

and *The Secret War of Harry Frigg* (1967, Jack Smight) are two large-scale comedies with a few small-scale laughs between them. The best is the scene of staged warfare in the former film, with over-enthusiastic Italian combatants insisting on "dying" a dozen times over—an unoriginal gag, but well-timed. *Up from the Beach* (1965, Robert Parrish) has, despite an obtrusive "love interest," a strong feeling of actuality that is missing from the all-star *The Longest Day,* and gains in tension by its modest brevity. Most striking of all is Cornel Wilde's *Beach Red* (1967), where the sheer strength of the director's sincerity carries all before it. The subject is the assault on a Pacific island held by the Japanese—the theme is uncompromisingly anti-war. If nothing very new is said, at least the old truths are restated with power and an invigorating lack of compromise. In its period and climate, this is one of that small handful of films that can fairly claim to have been bravely made.

The First World War was represented by a mediocre rehash of *A Farewell to Arms* (1957, Charles Vidor) and Stanley Kubrick's *Paths of Glory* (1958). The latter is an attack on the corruption, cruelty and arrogance among high-ranking military. Unfortunately it is soft in the centre. Beneath its outward sharp cynicism is an uneasy sentimentality, and for all its revelation of scum at the top, it is itself

Cornel Wilde and Rip Torn in the former's uncompromising production **BEACH RED.**

Kirk Douglas in PATHS OF GLORY.

fairly superficial. The casting of a famous star contributes to this uneasy sense of compromise: war would not be so awful if nice Kirk Douglas were in charge instead of nasty Adolphe Menjou.

*　*　*

From Russia came the ingratiating tragi-comedy *The Cranes Are Flying* (*Letyat zhuravli*, 1957, Mikhail Kalatozov), a lyrical drama of love and separation in sharp contrast to the majority of exported Soviet war films; also, the less memorable *Normandie-Niemen* (1959, Jean Dréville), made jointly with France and concerned with a Free French air squadron in Russia. Poland's *Lotna* (1959, Andrzej Wajda) once more revealed the country's deep-driven agony, in a story of brave but futile resistance to the Nazi invasion; and Jerzy Zarzycki's *The White Bear* (*Biały niedźwiedź*, 1959) forcefully depicted the uncertainty of life in an occupied town—personified by a Jew who escapes from a train on the way to a concentration camp and manages to exist in hiding dressed in a bear skin. The very grotesqueness of the disguise—though perfectly understandable within the confines of the story—adds to the chill terror and madness lurking below the surface of even the quietest moments. The Italian *Four Days of Naples* (*Le quattro giornate di Napoli*, 1962, Nanni Loy) and *Battle for*

'A lyrical drama of love and separation' from Russia: THE CRANES ARE FLYING.

Italy in 1943: a scene from FOUR DAYS OF NAPLES.

Robert Mitchum does his bit in THE BATTLE FOR ANZIO.

Anzio (1969, Edward Dmytryk, a joint production with America) are moderately efficient dramatic reconstructions—the Naples days are in September 1943, when the Germans were attempting to stiffen the weakening Italian resistance to the advancing Allies. Both films have their full share of *clichés,* but the first in particular is at times both moving and tense. Germany, at length recovering from breast-beating *ecce peccavi,* presented their side of the Stalingrad horror in *Battle Inferno* (1959, Frank Wisbar).

From France, Jean Renoir's *The Vanishing Corporal* (*Le caporal épinglé,* 1961), though again dealing with three contrasting characters, is in very different style from *La grande illusion* of the Thirties—a comedy of escaping prisoners with an emphasis on the friendships forged by wartime togetherness and doomed to be broken when peace returns. Despite a certain similarity of theme, this is clearly a picture made when no war-clouds were thought to gather. In some respects it is almost an affectionate parody of the overplayed P-O-W theme. Georges Franju's *Thomas the Imposter* (*Thomas l'imposteur,* 1964) is set in the First World War. Based on a novel by Jean Cocteau, it deals with the fantasy life of the nephew of a great general, and points the contrast between the superficial trappings and the underlying realities of war. The young man's pretence is used by a Polish princess to bring convoys of wounded to her mansion which she is intending

A scene from Georges Franju's strangely haunting THOMAS THE IMPOSTER.

to use as a hospital. The events consequent on this lead to his death at the Front from a sniper's bullet. From France/Japan came the famous and influential *Hiroshima mon amour* (1959, Alain Resnais, from a script by Marguerite Duras), dealing with the effects of war and the memories of war, and the essential need to forget. A young woman who has had a tragically concluded love affair with a German soldier finds the circumstances recalled to memory by her awareness of the Hiroshima shame (she is there to prepare an anti-war film) and by her meeting and brief relationship with a Japanese architect. Finally she parts from him—she will forget her personal tragedy together with the events that have revived it for her. On a first viewing the film is an intriguing—and intensely moving—puzzle. On a second its impact is overwhelming. Thereafter, and with the passing of the years, it oddly seems to lose power. This may well be its most subtle implication—that the first memories of the film itself become blurred and eventually fade.

* * *

Apart from Frédéric Rossif's documentary, *Mourir à Madrid*, two films touch on the Spanish Civil War, both set some years after the conflict and both concerned with ex-Republican sympathisers working

TO DIE IN MADRID: the civilian population experiences the horrors of war.

The sniper awaits his prey: Anthony Quinn in Fred Zinnemann's BEHOLD A PALE HORSE.

from France. Fred Zinnemann's *Behold a Pale Horse* (1964) is a straightforward conventional story of revenge. *La guerre est finie* (1966, Alain Resnais, made jointly with Sweden), on the other hand, is a subtle study of despairing resignation, of tired acceptance of defeat—of money and forgetfulness. Yves Montand gives an outstanding performance as the courier for a group of Spanish communists in exile who finds himself apart both from his older associates and from the young revolutionary generation of starry-eyed romanticists. With a total knowledge of their uselessness, he goes through the actions required of him with a sort of grey scepticism. Once again Resnais is concerned with memory and time, blending past and present—and chillingly suggesting future—in a compelling if depressing picture of another kind of aftermath. The events depicted point the irony in the

126

title, and the film, France's entry for the 1966 Cannes Festival, was withdrawn following reactions from the Spanish government.

The Franco-Algerian struggle is the subject of Gillo Pontecorvo's *Battle of Algiers* (*La battaglia di Algèri*, 1965, an Algerian/Italian joint production), in which the director, though it is apparent where his sympathies lie, makes an effort to be fair to both sides. At least he shows that the "dedicated revolutionary" can behave with as much vileness as any oppressor, and that in the long run there is not a great deal to choose between the advocates of violence whatever they profess to represent. The ruthless, bawling, almost inhuman faces of some of the demonstrating crowds in their hour of triumph or fury are as sinister a spectacle as any dictator's parade.

Turning back to earlier lunacies, Napoléon turns up again in Abel Gance's *Austerlitz* (1960), and also in the super-mammoth four-part *War and Peace* from Russia (*Voyna i mir*, 1963–7, Sergey Bondarchuk). Gance's infatuation for his "hero" finally overcomes all else, even the avoidance of stupefying tedium, and the result is as tawdry and depressing a spectacle as the cheapest and most costly Hollywood

Ingrid Thulin and Yves Montand in Resnais's LA GUERRE EST FINIE.

costume piece. That Napoléon comes across as a ranting bore may well be an ironically accurate portrayal, but was probably against the director's intention; it is only fair to say that the usual execrable dubbing may have been partly responsible for this fiasco. Bondarchuk's *War and Peace* is mainly memorable for the Battle of Borodino—which, though an unconscionable time a-coming, looks magnificent (and goes on for ever) when it finally does appear. And magnificent it should be, with apparently the entire Soviet armed forces at its disposal. At the end of a full and exhausting day's work one has seen some strikingly beautiful (and some extremely muddy) photography, one enchanting (Lyudmila Savyeleva) and several sound performances, and very little of Tolstoy except the bare bones of his vast plot. The English version, however, has not only been severely cut, but also, it appears, re-edited, so perhaps the great writer's message disappeared somewhere *en route*. The dubbing of the voices is even more abysmal than usual—indeed, the film contains a prime extract

The spectacular Battle of Borodino sequence from the Russian mammoth WAR AND PEACE.

128

for any anti-dubber's anthology, when a band of soldiers, after conversing in homely American accents, suddenly burst into perfect Russian song. In the old days, when the action was interspersed with captions from start to finish, the cinemas were crowded. It is surely time for the industry to realise that people have not lost the ability to read just because the titles of today have to appear lower down on the screen.

Napoléon is also present by implication in Georges Franju's fine short, *Hôtel des Invalides* (1951), in which the unpleasant contents of the French war museum are used with trenchant irony as the basis for a devastating attack on the false glamour of militarism, and in particular the loathsome conjunction of carnage and church. Less powerful, but an interesting technical experiment, is the British/Russian *1812* (1965, Stan Strangeway), an 18-minute short depicting Napoléon's Moscow campaign by the use of model soldiers, set to Tchaikovsky's "Overture" and intercut with Second World War newsreels. Parts of the film are confusing, particularly the presence of a (real) woman dressed in black and gazing out across the water. For most of its brief length, however, this is a gripping and original little work. Toys were put to brilliant use also in a Canadian 8-minute short of that title (*Toys*, 1966) directed by Grant Munro. It opens with happy children gazing at a shop window full of various models. Suddenly the little animals and other toys come to life before their delighted eyes. Attention is then turned to a collection of military models—tanks, guns, soldiers, aircraft—ranged on a little battlefield, which also begin to move and, before the increasingly apprehensive faces of the children, embark on a battle of horrifying intensity. The din of death and destruction mounts to a fearful climax as a soldier writhes on the ground, burnt by napalm. Then once again everything is motionless, and we—and the children—are gazing silently into a shop window. There could be no more pertinent comment on human folly, and we remind ourselves that a movie camera itself is essentially a toy—and only too often irresponsibly used as one where war is concerned.

Nothing worthy of note on the American Civil War appeared from its own country, but a fine short arrived from France in Robert Enrico's *Incident at Owl Creek* (*La rivière du Hibou*, 1961) from a short story by Ambrose Bierce. It deals with the execution of a partisan by hanging from a bridge high over a river, and his imagined escape and return home to his wife in the split second before the rope tightens round his neck. A beautifully graduated exercise in the progress from joyous release, through gradually increasing unease to final

The opening sequence from Robert Enrico's fine short, INCIDENT AT OWL CREEK.

Stanley Baker and unnamed warrior in ZULU.

horror, the film is also as meaningful a parable as any about the straw-clutching hopes of men caught up in a grim, inescapable reality.

Three British Empire spectaculars appeared: *Zulu* (1963, Cy Endfield), *Khartoum* (G.B./U.S.A., 1966, Basil Dearden) and *The Charge of the Light Brigade* (1968, Tony Richardson). The first is merely a present-day blockbuster set back a little—comic relief, brief moments of beautifully photographed military hell—a fairly disagreeable piece of film-making. *Khartoum,* the best of the trio, ingeniously mixes truth and whitewash: cast Charlton Heston as Gordon and you are half-way home. Plenty of famous names appear as other famous names, but the net result, despite the killing, is dull. *The Charge of the Light Brigade* at least attempts to lambast the criminal stupidity, callousness and pomposity of certain military leaders, but as these are well-known today it seems an expensive way of repeating platitudes. Perhaps the famous Brigade can now be considered to have charged to a halt.

The Vietnamese War, cutting across American life and conscience

THE CHARGE OF THE LIGHT BRIGADE from Tony Richardson's version.

131

John Wayne, staunch and reliable in THE GREEN BERETS.

like a deep wound, inspired film-makers to only one large-scale production, John Wayne's notorious justification *The Green Berets*
(1968). In the state of feeling prevalent on its release it aroused, not
unexpectedly, storms of protest. As one British critic remarked, the
unpleasantness of the film was equalled by the repulsiveness of the
demonstrators jeering delightedly every time an American soldier was
killed. Viewed away from partisan passion, the film appears no more
and no less nauseating than the great majority of propagandist war
pictures. The same bloody action scenes, the same loaded dialogue,
the same contrived sentimental situations, the same dreadful soft-
centred toughness. In fact, bearing in mind once more the climate
of its time, it could be said that *The Green Berets* is a somewhat more
courageous production than similar epics issued when all opposition

*Grim determination all round: Wayne, Irene Tsu and Jack Soo in THE
GREEN BERETS.*

is silenced or all public opinion in favour. At the very least, one can have little doubt as to its maker's sincerity.

Sincerity no doubt also inspired the French multi-part documentary *Far from Vietnam* (*Loin du Viêt-Nam*, 1967), financed as it was by its makers, Alain Resnais, William Klein, Joris Ivens, Agnès Varda, Claude Lelouch, and Jean-Luc Godard, and it is perhaps not surprising that such a film should come from its source. There is, howhowever, sincere or not, a smugness, a self-righteousness about this scrappy anthology directed against another country's dilemma, without any real attempt to understand it, that renders the film—especially when looked back on today—as oddly ineffective and contrived as the pro-war apologia itself. Vague shapes of beams and motes, of pots and kettles, moreover, hover through the fog and filthy air.

Godard's contemptible pantomime parody in *Pierrot le fou* (1965) is best forgotten.

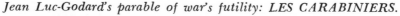

Two films set in imaginary wars were Godard's *Les carabiniers* (1963) and Ingmar Bergman's *Shame* (*Skammen*, 1968). The former concerns two loutish farm-workers called up to serve their King in

Jean Luc-Godard's parable of war's futility: LES CARABINIERS.

134

some vague, never-defined war. They are told by the military police what a wonderful time they will have, and the film then proceeds to show them indulging in a sleep-walking orgy of cruelty and slaughter. They return home to their lumpish women and pour out piles of postcards showing the beautiful and wonderful places and scenes they have visited—all to be theirs after the enemy's unconditional surrender. What they do, in fact, receive is summary execution (by the same military police who first called them up), the country's ruler having been toppled from his throne by a revolution. Despite the director's usual casual, coolly detached approach (which is apt to leave the spectator feeling "if you care so little why should we care more?") the film is at least a fresh presentation of an old truth, even if the postcard-pouring scene (admittedly a cheap way of using up screen time) is protracted to exasperating lengths.

Bergman's *Shame* is not, in the strict sense, a "war" film: in fact, the war is treated almost as a natural disaster—the soldiers and officials engaged in it go about their business as uncomprehendingly as the hapless civilians who are herded this way and that. It is, rather, a study of the depths to which anyone might sink to survive, and at the

The closing sequence from Ingmar Bergman's horrifying and masterly SHAME.

Liv Ullmann, unforgettable in SHAME.

same time a comment on the inefficacy of the artist (musician, film-maker, or whoever) in a world where there are no ivory towers that cannot be blown up. Ultimately, we are all ready to betray to live—to betray again. So complex a masterpiece cannot be adequately discussed in a few lines. On the purely superficial level, the physical terror of bombardment has never been more graphically conveyed than in the brief scene where the ex-violinist and his wife scrabble for cover in their cottage; at the other extreme, the final shots of the wretched, hopeless boat-load of would-be refugees trapped for all time in a great floating mass of corpses may well be the last word on the human condition.

*   *   *

Finally, the early and mid-Sixties were remarkable for a spate of awful-warning productions as the bomb-race gathered ever more threatening speed. Starting with *On the Beach* (U.S.A., 1959, Stanley Kramer), through the highlights of *Dr Strangelove, or How I Learned to Stop Worrying and Love the Bomb* (G.B., 1964, Stanley Kubrick),

Watching the progress of doom: one of the fantastic sets from DOCTOR STRANGELOVE

Fail-Safe (U.S.A., 1964, Sidney Lumet), *The Bedford Incident* (G.B., 1965, James B. Harris) and *The War Game* (G.B., 1965, Peter Watkins), one after another, with increasing grimness and in widely differing styles, demonstrated the case with which disaster might be precipitated. *On the Beach,* which foresaw the destruction of the Northern Hemisphere by nuclear war in 1964, and the consequent drifting of lethal radiation to the rest of the world, has its message vitiated by banal personal relationships and by a general lack of bite in the way in which the whole warning system is put over. There is also the falsely reassuring use once more of those familiar faces. Despite several powerfully disturbing scenes one is left feeling at the end that radiation might come, but at least there will be Ava Gardner to cheer the final hours. Of the rest, *Dr. Strangelove* is the bitterest and most imaginative—with lunacy and incompetence ruling the world's end; *Fail-Safe* is the most relentlessly uncompromising—contemplating the murder of an entire capital city by one government to prove to another that it meant no harm; *The Bedford Incident* is the most uneasily possible—an armed confrontation that could arise any day through one man's arrogance or another's obstinacy; and *The*

Henry Fonda, right, as the harassed American President in FAIL SAFE.

War Game is the most immediately terrifying in its realism—a news-reel style reportage of an atomic attack on Britain, that was banned from television as being too upsetting. All have one attitude in common that differentiates them from the awful-warning products of earlier years—there is no enemy. There is only the common enemy of human error or mischance. Compared to a film such as *An Englishman's Home* this is something of an improvement. It might even offer a gleam of hope—a plea for constructive thought to offset the mindless ranting of so many "war films" that have sullied the cinema screen.

Satire and ridicule: above—M*A*S*H.; below—HOW I WON THE WAR.

9. M*A*S*H and Beyond

WITH THE ADVENT of *M*A*S*H* (1969, Robert Altman—the initials stand for Mobile Army Surgical Hospital), the war film seemed to achieve a sort of catharsis. Except for one or two productions already in the making there was a noticeable easing-off following its appearance, which has continued to the present day. Why this particular film, set in Korea, should have had this effect is not easy to discover. It may, indeed, be merely a neat coincidence—but there seems little doubt that *M*A*S*H* will have its influence on those to follow. Despite this, it is an anti-authority rather than an anti-war film—in fact it is in a sense pro-war, in that the authority defied or sabotaged is through its stupidity hindering the successful waging of the war by undermining the efficiency of an organisation (the hospital unit) whose insanely dual purpose is to save life and to patch lives up to be sent back for renewed destruction. In Richard Lester's *How I Won the War* (G.B., 1967) and, more successfully, Mike Nichols's *Catch-22* (U.S.A., 1970) the humour of the absurd is used to point the tragic idiocy of war; in *M*A*S*H* it is used rather to prove the necessity for men to pursue their chosen calling steadily through both the red-tape entanglements of inefficient officialdom and the stultifying barriers of petty discipline. Beneath the wild farce of a film made primarily for laughter is a sober reminder that in a world gone mad the prime duty of a sane man is—by whatever fantastical means he may have at his disposal—to preserve his own sanity.

Chief among a handful of American productions in more familiar mould during the recent period is Franklin J. Schaffner's *Patton* (*Patton—Lust for Glory*, 1969), in which a comparatively recent military leader is portrayed in colours that appear to be remarkably true. The appalling egotism, narrowness, conceit and arrogance of the military type of which Patton was no more than an outstanding example, are presented with a frankness that in earlier years would only have been accorded to the enemy. Particularly ingenious is the way in which on occasion an apparently sympathetic approach will be used ironically to strengthen the total impression. For once the inevitable choice of a star actor to play so star a part does not have the usual weakening effect, for George C. Scott's superb performance sinks his own personal image almost totally in the real-life character he portrays. The film may not be an overtly anti-war document, it is certainly a devastating exposure of a dedicated wager of war.

For the rest, *Kelly's Heroes* (1970, Brian G. Hutton) is a nasty

The famous slapping scene: George C. Scott as PATTON.

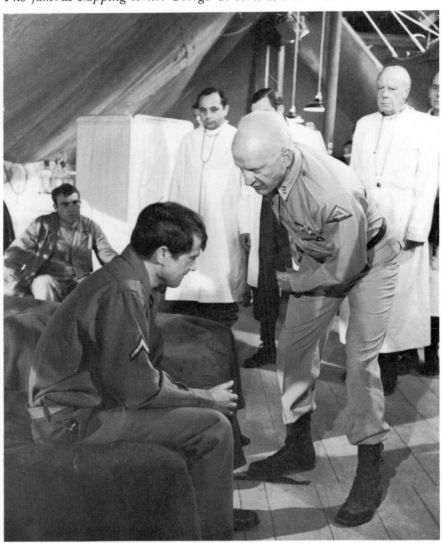

piece of noisy nullity, delighting in its own violence, with none of the witty burlesque of the same director's *Where Eagles Dare*; *The Last Escape* (1969, Walter Grauman) is routine adventure material, interesting only because of the extraordinary—and surely unintended—light it casts on America's integrity in regard to her Allies, as the Russians then were. *Too Late the Hero* (1969, Robert Aldrich) is also shoddy stuff—a dirty Half Dozen in the Philippines with the usual quota of violence (lovingly lingering shot of soldier hung upside down by wicked Japanese). That it deals with British rather than American troops is almost the only change to record. It could have been made (and indeed has only too often been made) at any time during the past twenty years; if it had never been made at all the loss to the cinema would have been nil. *Murphy's War* (1971, Peter Yates) concerns one man's determination to carry on his private war even after the public one is officially concluded. Superficially an exciting action story about the hunt for a U-boat in the reaches of the Orinoco river in Venezuela, the film is also a revelation of the dubious motives,

Action in **TOO LATE THE HERO.**

The escape from the sinking ship in MURPHY'S WAR.

underlying the declared ones of righteous revenge and justified self-preservation, that may impel man to wage war even to the point of self-destruction. *Tora! Tora! Tora!* (1970, Richard Fleischer) was co-produced with Japan—a massive, unbiased epic of Pearl Harbor and the events immediately following. The action darts a little disconcertingly to and fro between either side, but the film is courageous in facing the not often faced facts leading up to the lamentable disaster. As a spectacle it is spotty: one dutifully admires the cleverness of the model work, as in *The Dam Busters* years before, but such admiration is in itself a criticism of something that should not be noticeable. The final shot is of the Japanese admiral gazing apprehensively across the empty ocean and wondering what retribution may be in store. In a film made by a conjunction of former enemies twenty-five years after such fears had been fulfilled by the killing, burning and mutilation of thousands of human beings in the space of one moment's passing, this is not only a trite and contrived ending, but a sickening one—a

144

smug reminder by the victor, where there should be only a common
shame.

*   *   *

Britain, during this same recent period, has relied almost wholly
on "battles long ago": *Cromwell* (1970, Ken Hughes) could well become, in fact, a classic example of how to misrepresent a famous one—
in this instance Naseby. All schoolchildren taken to see this U-Cer-
tificate film should be presented with a corrective history-book as they
leave the cinema. *The Adventures of Gerard* (1970, a joint production
of Britain, Italy and Switzerland, based on English stories and directed by a Pole—Jerzy Skolimowski—with Italian, British and American actors) is a vastly enjoyable Napoléonic romp derived from Sir

*Eli Wallach as Napoléon in THE ADVENTURES OF GERARD—based
on Conan Doyle's well-known adventure stories.*

Arthur Conan Doyle's famous creation, with a Little Corporal far more credible than that portrayed in Sergey Bondarchuk's stuffy *Waterloo* (1970), which even the vital personality of Rod Steiger cannot bring to life. It is difficult to believe that these two films had the same chief scriptwriter—H. A. L. Craig. In *Waterloo,* apart from one or two moments of unnecessary camera gimmickry the big battle itself is well-staged. For the rest, one watches the well-known figures posing in their hired costumes and waits with apprehensive certainty for the requisite *bons mots* to arrive on cue. Napoléon may be one of the most overrated characters in history, but the cinema has certainly done its best to redress the balance.

The Boer War is touched on briefly in *Young Winston* (1972, Richard Attenborough), but only in so far as it concerned the early Churchill. It seems doubtful whether that traumatic conflict will ever receive full and truthful representation on the screen—for which, perhaps, we should be thankful.

*   *   *

From a formidable combination of Russia, Poland, Yugoslavia, East Germany and Italy came *The Great Battle (Osvobozhdyeniye,* 1969, Yuri Ozerov), a stranded whale of a film about the German assault on Kursk in 1943 following the collapse of the Stalingrad offensive. It features the familiar, paternal, teddy-bear Stalin quietly and confidently (and, also, a little complacently) keeping everything under control with a quiet word here, a pointing finger there; the familiar battle-bashing; the familiar "human interest"; the familiar ghastly dubbing. The English version of some three hours is extracted from an original over three times as long. And in 1923 *Greed* was regarded as a monster!

*   *   *

Finally, three pictures of the First World War: from Britain the quickly disposable *Zeppelin* (1971, Etienne Périer), a sad waste of a potentially interesting subject (air-ship raids over Britain) set in 1915, and spending most of its time with the familiar double-bluffing spy and wooden-headed foe; from America *Von Richthofen and Brown* (1971, Roger Corman), and in the same year Dalton Trumbo's brilliant and horrifying *Johnny Got His Gun.* For Britain, the former was renamed *The Red Baron,* a less suitable title, for what lifts the film above the level of just another air ace tale is the relationship it

146

More Russian spectacle (aided by Poland, Yugoslavia, East Germany and Italy): THE GREAT BATTLE.

portrays between the German aviator and the man who shot him down and opened the road to Hermann Goering. The parallels and contrasts are entertainingly pointed and the production has plenty of the Corman flair—disarmingly reminding us in its treatment from time to time of his great horror film days.

Johnny Got His Gun is the last war film of any significance to appear to date, and takes its place among the very finest. It opens, behind the titles, with newsreels of the First World War, the rulers, generals, politicians, soldiers, accompanied by a bare and ominous drumbeat score. As the titles come to an end the screen is blacked out by a tremendous explosion—a shell landing in a crater where a young infantryman is crouched. When next we see him he lies on a hospital bed, faceless, blind, deaf, paralysed, bound like a mummy, able only to move his head slightly from side to side—treated by the authorities as a miracle of survival and a most interesting medical case. Through the devoted help of the one nurse who looks on him as a

147

human being rather than a specimen for experiment, he manages, by superhuman efforts, to achieve a spark of communication with the world once again. Regarded as something almost unbelievable, this tremendous inch forward is greeted with great excitement by the authorities. Then they discover that his magnificent achievement has only one purpose—he wishes to be exhibited to the world as an example of what the dreadful work of the power politicians and the war lords can result in. This does not suit them at all. Official pressure is brought to bear—the young man is shut up again in darkness and silence. All this part of the film is in black-and-white—throughout it are threaded flashbacks of his past life, beliefs, fears and hopes, related in a mixture of fact and fantasy, and photographed deliberately and ingeniously in colours prettified by memory: the memories of a very ordinary young man, all he has left and therefore brighter and warmer than the reality probably justified. The points made in this film have been made before, but seldom if ever with such devastating force. As it moves relentlessly to its ironic close it extends its bounds of refer-

Timothy Bottoms in Dalton Trumbo's devastating indictment, JOHNNY GOT HIS GUN; "a masterpiece of its kind."

A realistic trench scene from JOHNNY GOT HIS GUN.

ence to become a total indictment of man's inhumanity to man, whether on the battlefield or in a clinically impersonal hospital ward. But if it was this alone the film might be merely a depressing experience, an expression of glum, if indignant, pessimism. On the contrary, it is illuminated with compassion, containing as it does one of the most moving performances to be seen in the cinema, from Diane Varsi as the sympathetic nurse—as lonely in her way as he is himself—who with infinite pains and care leads him back along the path to some sort of life. The film is unquestionably a masterpiece of its kind—consequently it enriches the screen of one small cinema for a week or so, and is then thrust into oblivion.

"One of the most moving performances to be seen in the cinema": Diane Varsi in JOHNNY GOT HIS GUN.

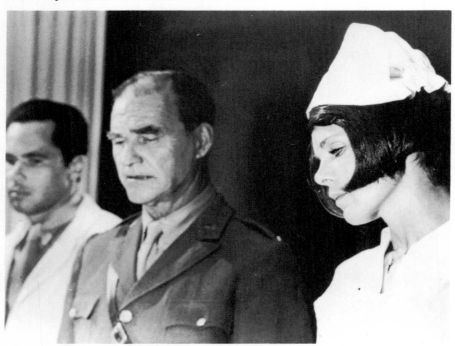

Epilogue—or Epitaph?

SO WE ARE LEFT, after seventy years' hard labour in the field of war, with a handful of great films, a couple of handfuls of fine ones, and fistfuls of mediocrity, or worse. Perhaps, after all, the proportions are not much worse than in any other film *genre*—or any other art form—and it may be that not the least powerful condemnation of war is in the amount of rubbish it produces in the cinema.

The future of the war films is even less predictable than that of other subjects. Production of sex-and-violence sagas steadily mounts as graphs of audience attendance steadily decline, but on the war front there appears at the moment to be something of a lull. One thing seems reasonably certain—massive "tributes" to this or that fighting force are becoming too expensive and are being dropped—one must be reasonable, after all, even in paying homage. For this reason *Tora! Tora! Tora!* apparently marks the last of the epics. Penury has its compensations.

Herbert Lom as Napoléon in the American WAR AND PEACE, directed by King Vidor. Mel Ferrer on the left.

Battle panorama from Bondarchuk's WAR AND PEACE.

Chronological List of War Films

IN THE FOLLOWING PAGES titles are listed chronologically under the seven most frequently filmed wars, with a final brief section on the Atomic Threat. The list is restricted to those concerned directly with the fighting, and to events closely connected with the conflict and its immediate aftermath. Most of the films included are already mentioned in the main text, but a few additional titles appear with brief comments; when of special interest, other credits apart from the director are given. While not claiming to be a complete list it is, I hope, a reasonably comprehensive record of the significant films in English or subtitled versions, good or bad, of each war concerned.

The Napoleonic Wars (c. 1803-15)

1910   **Roland the Grenadier (Il granatiere Rolland).** *Dir:* Arrigo Frusta.
1913   **The Battle of Waterloo.** *Dir:* Charles Weston.
1913   **The Napoleonic Epic.** *Dir:* Alberto Abati.
1915   **Brigadier Gerard.** *Dir:* Will Barker.
1915   **War and Peace (Voyna i mir).** *Dir:* Yakov Protazanov.
1926   **Napoléon—vu par Abel Gance.** *Dir:* Abel Gance. *Players:* Antonin Artaud, Annabella.
1928   **Bolibar.** *Dir:* Walter Summers. *Players:* Elissa Landi, Jerrold Robertshaw.
1928   **Waterloo.** *Dir:* Karl Grune.
1944   **Kutuzov.** *Dir:* Vladimir Petrov.
1951   **Hôtel des Invalides.** *Dir:* Georges Franju.
1956   **War and Peace.** *Dir:* King Vidor. *Players:* Henry Fonda, Audrey Hepburn, Mel Ferrer, Herbert Lom, John Mills, Anita Ekberg.
1960   **Austerlitz.** *Dir:* Abel Gance.
1965   **1812.** *Dir:* Stan Strangeway.
1967   **War and Peace (Voyna i mir).** *Dir:* Sergey Bondarchuk. *Players:* Lyudmila Savyeleva, Sergey Bondarchuk, Vyacheslav Tikhonov, Viktor Stanitsin, Vladislav Strzhelchik.
1970   **The Adventures of Gerard.** *Dir:* Jerzy Skolimowski. Based on the short stories of Sir Arthur Conan Doyle. *Players:* Peter McEnery, Claudia Cardinale, Eli Wallach, Jack Hawkins.
1970   **Waterloo.** *Dir:* Sergey Bondarchuk. *Players:* Rod Steiger, Christopher Plummer, Orson Welles, Jack Hawkins, Virginia McKenna.

The American Civil War (1861-65)

1910 **The Dixie Mother.** Vitagraph. *Players:* Florence Turner, Carlyle Blackwell, Norma Talmadge.

1911 **The Battle.** *Dir:* D. W. Griffith.

1913 **The Battle of Gettysburg.** *Dir:* Mack Sennett.

1915 **The Birth of a Nation.** *Dir:* D. W. Griffith. Derived from the Rev. Thomas Dixon's "The Clansman" and "The Leopard's Spots." *Players:* Lillian Gish, Henry B. Walthall, Mae Marsh, Robert Harron, George Siegman.

1916 **The Crisis.** *Dir:* Colin Campbell. *Player:* Marshall Neilan.

1922 **Grandma's Boy.** *Dir:* Fred Newmeyer. *Player:* Harold Lloyd.

1926 **The General.** *Dir:* Clyde Bruckman, Buster Keaton. *Players:* Buster Keaton, Marian Mack, Glen Cavender, Jim Farley.

1939 **Gone with the Wind.** *Dir:* Victor Fleming. *Players:* Vivien Leigh, Clark Gable, Olivia de Havilland, Leslie Howard, Thomas Mitchell, Jane Darwell.

1951 **The Red Badge of Courage.** *Dir:* John Huston. *Players:* Audie Murphy, Bill Maulden, John Dierkes, Royal Dano.

1954 **The Raid.** *Dir:* Hugo Fregonese. *Players:* Van Heflin, Anne Bancroft.

1954 **A Time out of War.** *Dir:* Denis Sanders.

1956 **The Great Locomotive Chase.** *Dir:* Francis D. Lyon. *Players:* Fess Parker, Jeffrey Hunter, Jeff York.

1961 **Incident at Owl Creek (La rivière du Hibou).** *Dir:* Robert Enrico.

D. W. Griffith's THE BIRTH OF A NATION.

The First World War (1914-18)

1914   **By the Kaiser's Orders.** *Dir:* Will Barker.

1914   **Called to the Front.** Regent.

1914   **England Expects.** *Dir:* George Loane Tucker. *Players:* Jane Gail, Charles Rock.

1914   **The German Spy Peril.** *Dir:* Will Barker.

1914   **The Fringe of War.** *Dir:* George Loane Tucker.

1914   **The Great European War.** *Dir:* George Pearson.

1914   **It's a Long Way to Tipperary.** B & C Company.

1914   **Saving the Colours.** B & C Company.

1915   **The White Sister.** Essanay. *Player:* Viola Allen.

1915   **How Lieutenant Rose R. N. Spiked the Enemy's Guns.** Clarendon.

1915   **If England Were Invaded.** Gaumont.

1915   **Somewhere in France.** Regal.

1915   **Tommy Atkins.** Barker.

1915   **War Is Hell.** Produced by Mrs. Ethyle Batley.

1915   **The Coward.** *Dir:* Thomas Ince.

1915   **The Battle Cry of Peace.** *Dir:* J. Stuart Blackton. *Players:* Norma Talmadge, Charles Richman.

1915   **Unfit.** *Dir:* Cecil Hepworth.

1916   **War Brides.** *Dir:* Herbert Brenon. *Players:* Nazimova, Richard Barthelmess.

1916   **Civilization.** *Dir:* Thomas Ince.

1916   **The War Bride's Secret.** *Dir:* Kenean Buel.

1916   **The Fall of a Nation.** *Dir:* Bartley Cushing. *Player:* Percy Standing (as William Jennings Bryan). A pro-war howl by the author of "The Clansman" (*The Birth of a Nation*), the Rev. Thomas Dixon.

1916   **We French.** *Dir:* Rupert Julian. *Player:* Gale Kane. She plays a young French girl who helps an American soldier to escape from the Huns and is duly tortured. The pattern was to become drearily familiar.

1916   **The Battle of the Somme.** *Dir:* G. Malins, J. B. McDowell.

1917   **The Woman's Land Army.** *Dir:* Walter West.

1917   **Joan the Woman.** *Dir:* Cecil B. DeMille. *Players:* Geraldine Farrar, Hobart Bosworth, Wallace Reid, Raymond Hatton, Theodore Roberts.

1917   **The Little American.** *Dir:* Cecil B. DeMille. *Players:* Mary Pickford, Jack Holt, Hobart Bosworth, Raymond Hatton, Walter Long.

1917   **The Slacker.** *Dir:* Christy Cabanné. *Players:* Walter Miller, Emily Stevens.

1917   **Shame.** *Dir:* John W. Noble.

1917   **The Secret Game.** *Dir:* William C. DeMille. *Player:* Sessue Hayakawa, as an American-Japanese who helps his adopted country fight his native country in Russia.

1917   **The Greatest Power.** *Dir:* Edwin Carewe.

1917   **Arms and the Girl.** *Dir:* Josepf Kaufman. *Players:* Billie Burke, Thomas Meighan. An early war comedy not unlike the British *Mademoiselle from Armentières,* but with some grim torture scenes interpolated.

1917   **The Battle of Arras; The Battle of Ancre; St Quentin.** *Dirs:* G.
       Malins and J. B. McDowell.
1918   **Hearts of the World.** *Dir:* D. W. Griffith. *Players:* Lillian Gish,
       Dorothy Gish, Erich von Stroheim, Robert Harron, Noël Coward.
1918   **Till I Come Back to You.** *Dir:* Cecil B. DeMille. *Players:* Bryant
       Washburn, Florence Vidor, Monte Blue.
1918   **The Hun Within.** *Dir:* Chester Withey. Dorothy Gish, George
       Fawcett.
1918   **The Prussian Cur.** *Dir:* Raoul Walsh. An attack on disloyal German-
       Americans encouraging lynchings by a Klu-Klux-Klan-like organisa-
       tion. The film was later withdrawn.
1918   **The Unbeliever.** *Dir:* Alan Crosland.
1918   **Mrs. Slacker.** *Dir:* Hobart Henley. A wife is shamed by her mate's
       reluctance to join the fight.
1918   **The Kaiser's Shadow.** *Dir:* Thomas Ince. *Players:* Dorothy Dalton,
       Thurston Hall. Two German spies after an embryonic V-weapon.
1918   **I'll Say So.** *Dir:* Raoul Walsh. *Player:* George Walsh.
1918   **The Woman the Germans Shot.** *Dir:* John Adolfi. Nurse Edith
       Cavell—who else?—played by Julia Arthur.
1918   **My Four Years in Germany.** *Dir:* William Nigh.
1918   **The Kaiser—Beast of Berlin.** *Dir:* Rupert Julian—who also played
       the Hun King.
1918   **Shoulder Arms.** *Dir:* Charles Chaplin. *Players:* Charles Chaplin,
       Sydney Chaplin, Edna Purviance.
1918   **Kiddies in the Ruins.** *Dir:* George Pearson. *Player:* Sybil Thorndike.
1918   **The Invasion of Britain.** *Dir:* Herbert Brenon.
1919   **The Unpardonable Sin.** *Dir:* Marshall Neilan. *Players:* Blanche
       Sweet, Wallace Beery. The Germans committed it.
1919   **Comradeship.** *Dir:* Maurice Elvey. *Players:* Gerald Ames, Lily Elsie.
1919   **J'accuse!** *Dir:* Abel Gance.
1919   **Yankee-Doodle in Berlin.** *Dir:* Mack Sennett. *Player:* Ben Turpin
       type-cast as the Kaiser.
1920   **Humoresque.** *Dir:* Frank Borzage. *Player:* Gaston Glass, as the
       violinist whose career is endangered by the war.
1921   **How Lord Kitchener Was Betrayed.** *Dir:* Percy Nash.
1921   **The Four Horsemen of the Apocalypse.** *Dir:* Rex Ingram. *Script:*
       June Mathis, from the novel by V. Blasco Ibanez. *Players:* Rudolph
       Valentino, Alice Terry, Wallace Beery, Josef Swickard, Stuart
       Holmes.
1921   **The Battle of Jutland.** *Dir:* H. Bruce Woolfe.
1923   **Armageddon.** *Dir:* H. Bruce Woolfe.
1923   **The Hero.** *Dir:* Louis Gasnier. *Player:* Gaston Glass. An original
       little story about a man who is regarded with contempt when he
       returns from the war and does not sustain his military reputation.
1924   **Zeebrugge.** *Dir:* H. Bruce Woolfe.
1924   **Reveille.** *Dir:* George Pearson. *Players:* Betty Balfour, Stewart Rome,
       Ralph Forbes.
1924   **The Sideshow of Life.** *Dir:* Herbert Brenon. *Player:* Ernest Tor-
       rence, as a clown who finds it hard to return to clowning after

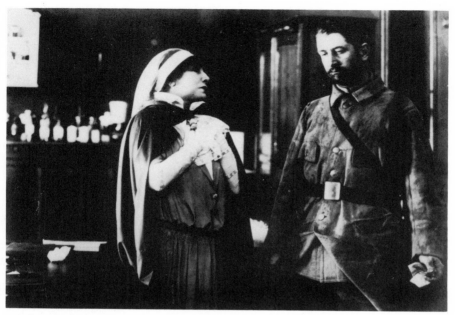

Sarah Bernhardt (above) appeared in a propaganda film in 1916, the title of which (MOTHERS OF FRANCE) is self-explanatory. The director was Louis Mercanton and the cast included Gabriel Signoret. Location sequences in the actual trenches were included.

being a general during the war. This is taken straight, instead of the devastating satire it might have been.

1924 **The Enchanted Cottage.** *Dir:* John S. Robertson. *Players:* Richard Barthelmess, May McAvoy.

1925 **Ypres.** *Dir:* Walter Summers.

1925 **The Big Parade.** *Dir:* King Vidor. From a story by Laurence Stallings. *Players:* Renée Adorée, John Gilbert, Hobart Bosworth, Karl Dane.

1926 **Mademoiselle from Armentières.** *Dir:* Maurice Elvey. *Players:* Estelle Brodie, John Stuart, Alf Goddard, Marie Ault.

1926 **Mare Nostrum.** *Dir:* Rex Ingram. *Players:* Antonio Moreno, Alice Terry. Submarine stuff.

1926 **Behind the Front.** *Dir:* Edward Sutherland. *Players:* Wallace Beery, Raymond Hatton. One of the best war comedies from a once-famous team.

1926 **What Price Glory?** *Dir:* Raoul Walsh. From the play by Laurence Stallings and Maxwell Anderson. *Players:* Edmund Lowe, Victor McLaglen, Dolores del Rio.

1926 **Mons.** *Dir:* Walter Summers.

1926 **Roses of Picardy.** *Dir:* Maurice Elvey. *Players:* Lillian Hall-Davis, John Stuart, Jameson Thomas.

1927 **Wings.** *Dir:* William Wellman. *Players:* Richard Arlen, Buddy Rogers, Jobyna Ralston, Clara Bow, Gary Cooper.

1927 **The Strong Man.** *Dir:* Frank Capra. *Player:* Harry Langdon. The early sequences take place at the front, with Chaplin-Laurel-Hardy-type comedy.

1927 **Battle of the Coronel and Falkland Islands.** *Dir:* Walter Summers.

1927 **Blighty.** *Dir:* Adrian Brunel. *Players:* Ellaline Terris, Jameson Thomas, Godfrey Winn, Wally Patch, Seymour Hicks, Renee and Billy Houston.

1927 **Verdun, visions d'histoire.** *Dir:* Léon Poirier.

1927 **The Emden.** Produced by the Emelka Company, Germany.

1927 **The Somme.** *Dir:* M. A. Wetherell.

1928 **Mademoiselle Parley-Voo.** *Dir:* Maurice Elvey. *Players:* Estelle Brodie, John Stuart, Alf Goddard.

1928 **Poppies of Flanders.** *Dir:* Arthur Maude. *Players:* Jameson Thomas, Eve Gray.

1928 **The Guns of Loos.** *Dir:* Sinclair Hill.

1928 **Dawn.** *Dir:* Herbert Wilcox. *Players:* Sybil Thorndike, Mary Brough, Haddon Mason.

1928 **Lilac Time.** *Dir:* George Fitzmaurice. *Players:* Gary Cooper, Colleen Moore.

1928 **Captain Swagger.** *Dir:* Edward H. Griffith. *Players:* Rod LaRocque, Sue Carol.

1928 **The Legion of the Condemned.** *Dir:* William Wellman. *Player:* Gary Cooper.

1928 **Q Ships.** *Dirs:* Geoffrey Barkas, Michael Barringer.

1929 **The Cock-Eyed World.** *Dir:* Raoul Walsh. *Players:* Victor McLaglen, Edmund Lowe, Lili Damita.

1929 **The Burgomaster of Stilemonde.** *Dir:* George Banfield. *Players:* Sir John Martin-Harvey, Fern Andra, Robert Andrews. A film version of the well-known play by Maurice Maeterlinck about German beastliness in Belgium.

1930 **All Quiet on the Western Front.** *Dir:* Lewis Milestone. *Script:* George Abbott and Maxwell Anderson, from Erich Maria Remarque's best-selling novel. *Players:* Lew Ayres, Slim Summerville, Louis Wolheim, Raymond Griffith.

1930 **The Dawn Patrol.** *Dir:* Howard Hawks. *Players:* Richard Barthelmess, Douglas Fairbanks Jr, Gladden James.

1930 **Westfront 1918.** *Dir:* G. W. Pabst.

1930 **Journey's End.** *Dir:* James Whale. *Players:* Colin Clive, David Manners, Billy Bevan, Anthony Bushell. A faithful rendering of R. C. Sherriff's famous play.

1930 **The W Plan.** *Dir:* Victor Saville. *Script:* Frank Launder. *Players:* Brian Aherne, Madeleine Carroll, Gordon Harker, Milton Rosmer.

1930 **Hell's Angels.** *Dir:* Howard Hughes. *Players:* Ben Lyon, James Hall, Jean Harlow, John Darrow. James Whale, dialogue director, assisted Hughes on this epic.

Léon Poirier's VERDUN—VISIONS D'HISTOIRE.

1931 **Tell England.** *Dir:* Anthony Asquith. *Players:* Carl Harbord, Tony Bruce, Wally Patch, Fay Compton. The script was taken from Ernest Raymond's best-seller of the same name.

1931 **Hell on Earth (Niemandsland).** *Dir:* Victor Trivas.

1931 **The Doomed Battalion (Berge in Flammen).** *Dir:* Luis Trenker.

1932 **Sky Devils.** *Dir:* Edward Sutherland.

1932 **The Man I Killed (Broken Lullaby).** *Dir:* Ernst Lubitsch. *Script:* Reginald Berkeley, from Maurice Rostand's play. *Players:* Phillips Holmes, Nancy Carroll, Lionel Barrymore, Lucien Littlefield, Tully Marshall, Zasu Pitts.

1932 **A Farewell to Arms.** *Dir:* Frank Borzage. *Players:* Gary Cooper, Helen Hayes, Adolphe Menjou. The first Ernest Hemingway novel to reach the cinema.

1932 **Pack Up Your Troubles.** *Dir:* George Marshall, Raymond McCarey. *Players:* Stan Laurel, Oliver Hardy. The first half of this L & H comedy, set at the front and climaxing with the capture by the two heroes of an entire enemy regiment, is by far the best part and indeed bids fair to equal Chaplin's *Shoulder Arms.*

1933 **I Was a Spy.** *Dir:* Victor Saville. *Players:* Madeleine Carroll, Conrad Veidt.

1933 **Morgenrot.** *Dir:* Gustav Ucicky.

1933 **The Eagle and the Hawk.** *Dir:* Stuart Walker. *Player:* Fredric March.

1933 **Ace of Aces.** *Dir:* J. W. Ruben. *Players:* Richard Dix, Mary Astor.

159

1935 **Brown on Resolution (Forever England).** *Dir:* Walter Forde. Script adapted from C. S. Forrester's novel. *Players:* John Mills, Betty Balfour, Jimmy Hanley, Barry Mackay.

1936 **Sons o' Guns.** *Dir:* Lloyd Bacon. *Player:* Joe E. Brown. Knockabout war comedy which depends entirely on the individual viewer's opinion of the large-mouthed comic involved.

1936 **The Road to Glory.** *Dir:* Howard Hawks. *Players:* Fredric March, June Lang, Lionel Barrymore.

1937 **La grande illusion.** *Dir:* Jean Renoir. *Script:* Charles Spaak, Jean Renoir. *Players:* Jean Gabin, Pierre Fresnay, Erich von Stroheim, Dalio.

1938 **Submarine Patrol.** *Dir:* John Ford. *Players:* Richard Greene, Nancy Kelly, Preston Foster. Lifted a little from the submarine warfare film bed by the director's touch.

1939 **Nurse Edith Cavell.** *Dir:* Herbert Wilcox. *Players:* Anna Neagle, George Sanders, Edna May Oliver.

1939 **The Hostages (Les otages).** *Dir:* Raymond Bernard. *Players:* Charpin, Saturnin Fabre.

1939 **We're in the Army Now.** *Dir:* Terry Morse.

1939 **Enemy Agent.** *Dir:* Terry Morse.

1941 **Sergeant York.** *Dir:* Howard Hawks. *Players:* Gary Cooper, Walter Brennan, Joan Leslie, Stanley Ridges.

1958 **A Farewell to Arms.** *Dir:* Charles Vidor. *Players:* Rock Hudson, Jennifer Jones. A final farewell, we may hope.

1958 **Paths of Glory.** *Dir:* Stanley Kubrick.

1962 **Lawrence of Arabia.** *Dir:* David Lean. *Script:* Robert Bolt. *Players:* Peter O'Toole, Alec Guinness, Anthony Quinn, Jack Hawkins, José Ferrer.

1964 **Thomas l'imposteur.** *Dir:* Georges Franju.

1966 **The Blue Max.** *Dir:* John Guillermin. *Players:* James Mason, George Peppard, Ursula Andress.

1968 **1917.** *Dir:* Stephen Weeks.

1969 **Oh! What a Lovely War.** *Dir:* Richard Attenborough. From the radio programme by Charles Chilton and the stage production by Joan Littlewood. *Players:* John Gielgud, Laurence Olivier, Michael Redgrave, Joe Melia, Jack Hawkins, Ralph Richardson, Kenneth More, Mary Wimbush, John Clements, Maggie Smith, John Mills, Cecil Parker, Susannah York, Dirk Bogarde, Jean-Pierre Cassel.

1971 **Zeppelin.** *Dir:* Etienne Périer. *Players:* Michael York, Elke Sommer, Marius Goring.

1971 **Von Richthofen and Brown (G.B.: The Red Baron).** *Dir:* Roger Corman. *Players:* John Phillip Law, Don Stroud, Barry Primus.

1971 **Johnny Got His Gun.** *Dir:* Dalton Trumbo. *Script:* Dalton Trumbo, from his own novel. *Players:* Timothy Bottoms, Diane Varsi, Jason Robards, Donald Sutherland.

The Spanish Civil War (1936-39)

1937 **The Spanish Earth.** *Dir:* Joris Ivens.

1937 **Heart of Spain.** *Dir:* Herbert Kline.

1938 **Blockade.** *Dir:* William Dieterle. *Players:* Henry Fonda, Madeleine Carroll.

1938 **Spanish ABC.** *Dir:* Thorold Dickinson.

1938 **L'espoir (Days of Hope).** *Dir:* André Malraux.

1939 **Spain.** *Dir:* Esther Shub.

1939 **L'assedio dell'Alcázar.** *Dir:* Augusto Genino.

1943 **For Whom the Bell Tolls.** *Dir:* Sam Wood. *Players:* Gary Cooper, Ingrid Bergman, Akim Tamiroff.

1950 **Guernica.** *Dir:* Alain Resnais.

1962 **Unbändiges Spanien (Untameable Spain).** *Dir:* Kurt Stern. The conflict through East German eyes.

1962 **Mourir à Madrid.** *Dir:* Frédéric Rossif.

1964 **Behold a Pale Horse.** *Dir:* Fred Zinnemann. *Players:* Gregory Peck, Anthony Quinn.

1966 **La guerre est finie.** *Dir:* Alain Resnais. *Players:* Yves Montand, Ingrid Thulin, Geneviève Bujold, Michel Piccoli.

The Second World War (1939-45)

1939 **The Lion Has Wings.** *Dir:* Michael Powell, Brian Desmond Hurst, Adrian Brunel. *Players:* Merle Oberon, Ralph Richardson.

1939 **The First Days.** *Dir:* Alberto Cavalcanti.

1940 **Bulldog Sees It Through.** *Dir:* Harold Huth.

1940 **Mystery Sea Raider.** *Dir:* Edward Dmytryk. *Player:* Jack Buchanan.

1940 **Night Train to Munich.** *Dir:* Carol Reed. *Players:* Margaret Lockwood, Rex Harrison, Paul Henreid.

1940 **Neutral Port.** *Dir:* Marcel Varnel.

1940 **London Can Take It.** *Dir:* Humphrey Jennings, Harry Watt.

1940 **Spring Offensive.** *Dir:* Humphrey Jennings.

1940 **Convoy.** *Dir:* Pen Tennyson. *Players:* Clive Brook, John Clements, Judy Campbell. A semi-documentary Navy film in which the "story," for once, is background to the factual detail. Pen Tennyson's skilful, restrained direction adds to one's regret for his early death.

1941 **The Seventh Survivor.** *Dir:* Leslie Hiscott. *Players:* Austin Trevor, Linden Travers. Fun and games with spies in a lighthouse.

1941 **A Yank in the R.A.F.** *Dir:* Henry King.

1941 **49th Parallel (U.S.: The Invaders).** *Dir:* Michael Powell. *Players:* Laurence Olivier, Leslie Howard, Anton Walbrook.

1941 **Next of Kin.** *Dir:* Thorold Dickinson. *Players:* Mervyn Johns, Stephen Murray, Nova Pilbeam.

1941 **Pimpernel Smith.** *Dir:* Leslie Howard. *Players:* Leslie Howard, Ronald Howard, Michael Rennie.

1941 **Dangerous Moonlight.** *Dir:* Brian Desmond Hurst. *Players:* Anton Walbrook, Sally Gray. Also the Warsaw Concerto, composed by Richard Addinsell.

1941 **Ships with Wings.** *Dir:* Sergey Nolbandov. *Players:* John Clements, Leslie Banks, Jane Baxter, Ann Todd. Naval drama based on the "Ark Royal," but the love affairs of the Vice-Admiral's daughter somewhat block the action.

1941 **Freedom Radio.** *Dir:* Anthony Asquith. *Players:* Clive Brook, Bernard Miles.

1941 **Target for Tonight.** *Dir:* Harry Watt.

1941 **Heart of Britain.** *Dir:* Humphrey Jennings.

1941 **Words for Britain.** *Dir:* Humphrey Jennings.

1941 **Listen to Britain.** *Dir:* Humphrey Jennings.

1942 **One of Our Aircraft Is Missing.** *Dir:* Michael Powell. *Players:* Godfrey Tearle, Eric Portman, Hugh Williams, Peter Ustinov, Googie Withers.

1942 **The Foreman Went to France.** *Dir:* Charles Frend. *Players:* Clifford Evans, Tommy Trinder, Constance Cummings.

1942 **In Which We Serve.** *Dir:* Noël Coward, David Lean. *Players:* Noël Coward, John Mills, Bernard Miles, Richard Attenborough, Celia Johnson, Michael Wilding, Kay Walsh.

1942 **The First of the Few.** *Dir:* Leslie Howard. *Players:* Leslie Howard, David Niven, Rosamund John.

1942 **Went the Day Well?** *Dir:* Alberto Cavalcanti. *Players:* Leslie Banks,

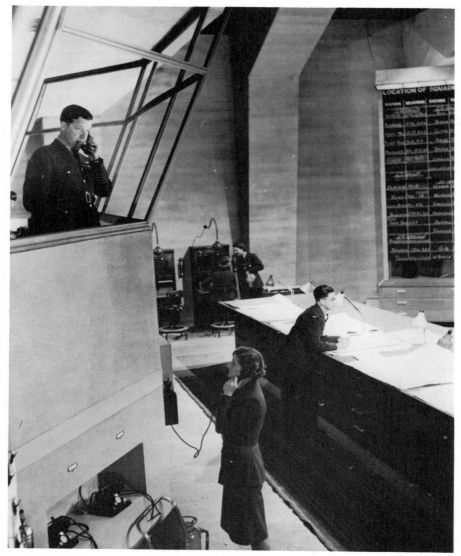

British documentary: COASTAL COMMAND.

Basil Sydney, Elizabeth Allen, Frank Lawton.

1942 **The Day Will Dawn.** *Dir:* Harold French.

1942 **Secret Mission.** *Dir:* Harold French.

1942 **Salute John Citizen.** *Dir:* Maurice Elvey.

1942 **Gert and Daisy Clean Up.** *Dir:* Maclean Rogers.

1942 **Back Room Boy.** *Dir:* Herbert Mason.

Women at war work: Patricia Roc and Megs Jenkins in MILLIONS LIKE US.

1942 **Coastal Command.** *Dir:* J. B. Holmes.

1942 **The Big Blockade.** *Dir:* Charles Frend.

1942 **This above All.** *Dir:* Anatole Litvak. *Players:* Tyrone Power, Joan Fontaine.

1942 **Mrs Miniver.** *Dir:* William Wyler. *Players:* Walter Pidgeon, Greer Garson, Teresa Wright.

1942 **To Be or Not to Be.** *Dir:* Ernst Lubitsch. *Players:* Jack Benny, Carole Lombard, Robert Stack, Felix Bressart, Lionel Atwill.

1942 **Parachute Nurse.** *Dir:* Charles Barton.

1942 **Wake Island.** *Dir:* John Farrow. *Players:* Brian Donlevy, Robert Preston, MacDonald Carey.

1942 **Bombs over Burma.** *Dir:* Joseph Lewis.

1942 **Air Force.** *Dir:* Howard Hawks. *Players:* John Garfield, Gig Young. Adventures of an American bomber in the Pacific. Sadly commonplace.

1942 **Squadron-Leader X.** *Dir:* Lance Comfort. *Players:* Eric Portman, Ann Dvorak, Martin Miller. An above-average adventure film about an ace German pilot sent on a mission in which he is to bail out over Belgium and spread false news about British bombing of civilian targets—a story enlivened by an outstanding performance from Eric Portman.

1942 **Casablanca.** *Dir:* Michael Curtiz. *Players:* Humphrey Bogart, Peter Lorre, Sydney Greenstreet, Ingrid Bergman.

1942-5 **Why We Fight (series).** *Dir:* Frank Capra. See page 69 for titles.

1942 **Natasha (Frontovyye podrugi).** *Dir:* V. Eisymont. One of the earliest war fiction films to appear in the West from Russia.

1943 **The Gentle Sex.** *Dir:* Leslie Howard. *Players:* Jean Gillie, Joan Gates, Rosamund John, Lilli Palmer.

1943 **Millions Like Us.** *Dir:* Frank Launder, Sidney Gilliat. *Players:* Eric Portman, Patricia Roc, Anne Crawford, Gordon Jackson, Megs Jenkins.

1943 **Fires Were Started.** *Dir:* Humphrey Jennings.

1943 **The Bells Go Down.** *Dir:* Basil Dearden.

1943 **The Silent Village.** *Dir:* Humphrey Jennings.

1943 **Flying Tigers.** *Dir:* David Miller. *Players:* John Wayne, Anna Lee. Routine Burmese melodrama—which a basis of truth does not make any more convincing than usual. A contemporary report warns that some of the fighting scenes might be unsuitable for "sensitive children."

1943 **Five Graves to Cairo.** *Dir:* Billy Wilder. *Players:* Franchot Tone, Anne Baxter, Erich von Stroheim. Along came Rommel—via E. von S.

1943 **Bataan.** *Dir:* Tay Garnett.

1943 **Sahara.** *Dir:* Zoltan Korda. *Players:* Humphrey Bogart, Lloyd Bridges, Bruce Bennett. Bogart as the Sergeant in the one (of many) about the isolated group of men.

1943 **Wings over the Pacific.** *Dir:* Phil Rosen.

1943 **Hitler's Children.** *Dir:* Edward Dmytryk. *Players:* Tim Holt, Bonita Granville.

1943 **Immortal Sergeant.** *Dir:* John Stahl. *Players:* Henry Fonda, Maureen O'Hara, Thomas Mitchell.

1943 **Lifeboat.** *Dir:* Alfred Hitchcock. *Players:* Tallulah Bankhead, William Bendix, Walter Slezak, John Hodiak, Henry Hull, Hume Cronyn. The script is based on a story by John Steinbeck.

1943 **Hitler's Madman.** *Dir:* Douglas Sirk. *Players:* Patricia Morison, Alan Curtis, John Carradine (as Heydrich) .

1943 **Bombers' Moon.** *Dir:* Charles Fuhr. *Players:* Annabella, George Montgomery. How Winston Churchill was saved from being blown up in a train through the good offices of an American pilot who stole a Messerschmidt.

1943 **The Silver Fleet.** *Dir:* Vernon Campbell Sewell, Gordon Wellesley.

War in the desert: Harry Watts's NINE MEN.

Players: Ralph Richardson, Googie Withers, John Longden, Esmond Knight. Above-average submarine drama with a Dutch setting, with reasonably credible situations and characters, and Richardson at his dignified best.

1943 **Victory through Air Power.** *Dir:* Walt Disney.

1943 **Nine Men.** *Dir:* Harry Watt. *Players:* Jack Lambert, Gordon Jackson, Grant Sutherland, Richard Wilkinson.

1943 **San Demetrio, London.** *Dir:* Charles Frend. *Players:* Walter Fitzgerald, Robert Beatty, Mervyn Johns, Ralph Michael, Gordon Jackson.

1943 **We Dive at Dawn.** *Dir:* Anthony Asquith. *Players:* John Mills, Eric Portman, Reginald Purdell.

1943 **Desert Victory.** *Dir:* Roy Boulting.

1943 **La bataille du rail.** *Dir:* René Clement.

1943 **The Story of Stalingrad.** Russian documentary reconstruction, with diagrams and maps.

1943 **The North Star.** *Dir:* Lewis Milestone. *Players:* Dana Andrews, Anne Baxter, Walter Huston, Anne Harding, Erich von Stroheim. A Hollywood "tribute" to the Russians, produced by Sam Goldwyn and written by Lillian Hellman, that caused more embarrassment—when relations became less cordial—than its mediocrity warranted. It was re-issued, in an "adapted" version, in 1957 as *Armored Attack*.

1943 **Battle for the Ukraine (Bitva na nashu sovyetskuyu Ukrainu).** *Dir:* Alexandr Dovzhenko.

1943 **Schweik's New Adventures.** *Dir:* Karel Lamac. *Players:* Lloyd Pearson, Julien Mitchell. The great humourous book of the First World War by the Czech Jaroslav Hašek has been most scurvily treated in this feeble updating. None of the hilarious satire remains, and all that is left is dismal farce.

1943 **The Life and Death of Colonel Blimp.** *Dir:* Michael Powell, Emeric Pressburger. *Players:* Roger Livesey, Deborah Kerr, Anton Walbrook. Cartoonist David Lows's bullying, swaggering, stupid military type has been softened into a lovable bumbler in this film version. The Second World War forms only a brief portion, but this is entertaining enough, and an occasional sharp point pierces the general amiability.

1944 **The Eighty Days.** *Dir:* Humphrey Jennings. A highly atmospheric documentary of the V1 attacks.

1944 **A Diary for Timothy.** *Dir:* Humphrey Jennings.

1944 **A Wing and a Prayer.** *Dir:* Henry Hathaway.

1944 **The Story of Dr. Wassell.** *Dir:* Cecil B. DeMille. *Players:* Gary Cooper, Laraine Day, Signe Hasso, Dennis O'Keefe, Paul Kelly.

1944 **The Purple Heart.** *Dir:* Lewis Milestone. *Player:* Dana Andrews.

1944 **Tunisian Victory.** Documentary compiled by the British and American Service Film Units.

1944 **The Battle of San Pietro.** *Dir:* John Huston.

1944 **Report from the Aleutians.** *Dir:* John Huston.

1944 **The Way Ahead.** *Dir:* Carol Reed. *Script:* Eric Ambler, Peter

167

Ustinov. *Players:* David Niven, William Hartnell, Raymond Huntley, Leslie Dwyer, Hugh Burden, John Laurie, Peter Ustinov, James Donald, Stanley Holloway, Jimmy Hanley.

1944   **The Rainbow (Raduga).** *Dir:* Mark Donskoy.

1944   **No Greater Love (Ona zashchishchayet Rodinu).** *Dir:* Fridrikh Ermler.

1945   **The Story of G.I. Joe.** *Dir:* William Wellman. *Players:* Burgess Meredith, Robert Mitchum.

1945   **They Were Expendable.** *Dir:* John Ford. *Players:* Robert Montgomery, John Wayne, Donna Reed.

1945   **Thirty Seconds over Tokyo.** *Dir:* Mervyn LeRoy. *Players:* Spencer Tracy, Van Johnson, Robert Walker. The script is by Dalton Trumbo, who, over twenty-five years later, was to make the fine First World War film *Johnny Got His Gun.*

1945   **Objective Burma.** *Dir:* Raoul Walsh. *Players:* Errol Flynn, James Brown, William Prince.

1945   **God Is My Co-Pilot.** *Dir:* Robert Florey. *Players:* Dennis Morgan, Dane Clark, Raymond Massey.

1945   **A Bell for Adano.** *Dir:* Henry King. *Players:* John Hodiak, Gene Tierney, William Bendix.

1945   **The Way to the Stars (U.S.: Johnny in the Clouds).** *Dir:* Anthony Asquith. *Players:* Michael Redgrave, John Mills, Rosamund John, Douglass Montgomery, Renée Asherson, Stanley Holloway, Trevor Howard. The keynote of the film, scripted by Terence Rattigan and Anatole de Grunwald, is John Pudney's poem, "Johnny Head-in-Air."

1945   **Burma Victory.** *Dir:* Roy Boulting.

1945   **The True Glory.** *Dir:* Carol Reed, Garson Kanin.

1945   **The Last Chance.** *Dir:* Leopold Lindtberg. *Players:* E. G. Morrison, John Hoy, Ray Reagan.

1945   **Berlin.** Russian newsreel-documentary, with commentary in English by A. Wistin.

1945   **Tomorrow Is Forever.** *Dir:* Irving Pichel. *Players:* Orson Welles, Claudette Colbert.

1945   **Rome—Open City (Roma, città aperta).** *Dir:* Roberto Rossellini. *Players:* Aldo Fabrizi, Anna Magnani, Maria Michi, Marcello Pagliero. Federico Fellini shared the script-writing with Sergio Amidei and Rossellini.

1946   **A Walk in the Sun.** *Dir:* Lewis Milestone. *Players:* Dana Andrews, Richard Conte.

1946   **Theirs Is the Glory.** *Dir:* Brian Desmond Hurst.

1946   **Paisà.** *Dir:* Roberto Rossellini. *Players:* Maria Michi, Carmela Sazio, Robert van Loon, Harriet White, Bill Tubbs, Gar Moore.

1946   **To Live in Peace (Vivere in pace).** *Dir:* Luigi Zampa. *Players:* Aldo Fabrizi, Gar Moore, Mirella Monti.

1946   **The Captive Heart.** *Dir:* Basil Dearden. *Players:* Michael Redgrave, Mervyn Johns, Basil Radford.

1946   **Tokyo Rose.** *Dir:* Lew Landers.

1946   **Madame Pimpernel.** *Dir:* Gregory Ratoff.

1946 **The Best Years of Our Lives.** *Dir:* William Wyler. *Players:* Fredric March, Myrna Loy, Dana Andrews, Teresa Wright, Harold Russell, Virginia Mayo.

1946 **The Turning Point (Veliki perelom).** *Dir:* Fridrikh Ermler. A fiction film based closely on events connected with the battle for Stalingrad.

1947 **The Search.** *Dir:* Fred Zinnemann. *Players:* Montgomery Clift, Wendell Corey, Ivan Jandl, Aline McMahon, Jarmila Novotna.

1947 **Frieda.** *Dir:* Basil Dearden. *Players:* Mai Zetterling, David Farrar. Adapted from Ronald Millar's play of the same name.

1947 **The Murderers Are amongst Us (Die Mörder sind unter uns).** *Dir:* Wolfgang Staudte. *Players:* Hildegarde Knef, Ernst Fischer.

1948 **Let There Be Light.** *Dir:* John Huston.

1948 **Jungle Patrol.** *Dir:* Joe Newman.

1948 **Fighter Squadron.** *Dir:* Raoul Walsh.

1948 **Command Decision.** *Dir:* Sam Wood.

1948 **The Boy with Green Hair.** *Dir:* Joseph Losey. *Players:* Dean Stockwell, Pat O'Brien, Robert Ryan, Barbara Hale.

1948 **Germany, Year Zero. (Germania anno zero).** *Dir:* Roberto Rossellini. *Players:* Edmund Moeschke, Ernest Pittschau, Ingetraut Hinze. Rossellini wrote the script in addition to directing this grim picture of life in the shattered capital.

1949 **The Third Man.** *Dir:* Carol Reed. *Script:* Graham Greene. *Players:* Orson Welles, Joseph Cotten, Alida Valli, Trevor Howard, Wilfrid Hyde-White, Bernard Lee.

THE THIRD MAN: Galloway (Trevor Howard) shows Holly Martins (Joseph Cotten) the results of Harry Lime's black-market operations.

1949   **Battleground.** *Dir:* William Wellman. *Players:* Van Johnson, John Hodiak, Ricardo Montalban, George Murphy, James Whitmore. The customary "group"—this time engaged in the Battle of the Bulge.

1949   **The Sands of Iwo Jima.** *Dir:* Allan Dwan. *Players:* John Wayne, John Agar, Forrest Tucker.

1949   **Twelve O'Clock High.** *Dir:* Henry King. *Players:* Gregory Peck, Dean Jagger, Gary Merrill, Hugh Marlowe.

1949   **Private Angelo.** *Dir:* Peter Ustinov. *Players:* Peter Ustinov, Godfrey Tearle, Robin Bailey, Maria Denis. The "unwilling soldier" theme is used to satirise gently, the sharp edge never being permitted to cut into the comedy, but the script, by Ustinov and Michael Anderson from Eric Linklater's novel, is pleasantly literate.

1950   **The Battle of Stalingrad (Stalingradskaya bitva).** *Dir:* Vladimir Petrov. Two-part fictionalised documentary, with the usual characterisations of Hitler, Stalin, *et al.* Plenty of noise, plus music by Khatchaturian.

1950   **The Men.** *Dir:* Fred Zinnemann. *Script:* Carl Foreman. *Players:* Marlon Brando, Teresa Wright, Everett Sloane.

1950   **The Halls of Montezuma.** *Dir:* Lewis Milestone. *Players:* Richard Widmark, Reginald Gardiner, Walter Palance, Karl Malden.

1950   **They Were Not Divided.** *Dir:* Terence Young. *Players:* Edward Underdown, Ralph Clanton, Helen Cherry.

1950   **The Wooden Horse.** *Dir:* Jack Lee. *Script:* Eric Williams from his own book. *Players:* Leo Genn, David Tomlinson, Anthony Steele, Bryan Forbes, Jacques Brunius, David Greene.

1950   **An American Guerilla in the Philippines (G.B.: I Shall Return).** *Dir:* Fritz Lang. The second title, taken from General MacArthur's remark after the Bataan defeat, is about all that rings true in this unfortunate slip of a famous director.

1950   **The Fall of Berlin (Padyeniye Berlina).** *Dir:* Mikhail Chiaureli. More Russian history-making, built round the romance of a young steel-worker whose girl is taken as prisoner to Germany when their home village is occupied. He ends up, however, helping to put the Red Flag on the Berlin Chancellory, meets his girl again among the crowds gathered to welcome the arrival of Stalin, and is paternally smiled upon by the great man himself.

1951   **Target Unknown.** *Dir:* George Sherman.

1951   **Decision before Dawn.** *Dir:* Anatole Litvak.

1951   **Flying Leathernecks.** *Dir:* Nicholas Ray.

1951   **The Desert Fox (G.B.: Rommel—Desert Fox).** *Dir:* Henry Hathaway. *Script:* Nunnally Johnson, from Desmond Young's biography. *Players:* James Mason, Cedric Hardwicke, Jessica Tandy, Luther Adler (as Hitler).

1951   **Force of Arms.** *Dir:* Michael Curtiz.

1951   **Up Front.** *Dir:* Alexander Hall. *Players:* David Wayne, Tom Ewell. Another good idea misfired. The film, based on Bill Mauldin's famous soldier cartoons, could have been a stimulatingly bitter satire—instead, a stock army farce of deadly familiarity.

170

1951 **You're in the Navy Now.** *Dir:* Henry Hathaway. *Players:* Gary Cooper, Jane Greer, Ray Collins. Rather engaging Navy comedy, with Cooper seemingly rather relieved at a change from his previous wartime Wassells and Yorks.

1952 **Okinawa.** *Dir:* Leigh Jason.

1952 **Thunder across the Pacific.** *Dir:* Allan Dwan.

1952 **Eight Iron Men.** *Dir:* Edward Dmytryk. *Players:* Bonar Colleano, Arthur Franz, Lee Marvin, Richard Kiley.

1952 **Angels One Five.** *Dir:* George More O'Ferrall. *Players:* Jack Hawkins, Andrew Osborn, Michael Denison, Cyril Raymond, John Gregson. An effective, small-scale section of the Battle of Britain story, in general avoiding the airpilot *clichés* to a commendable extent.

1952 **Les jeux interdits (Forbidden Games).** *Dir:* René Clément. *Players:* Brigitte Fossey, Georges Poujouly.

1952 **Neighbors.** *Dir:* Norman McLaren.

1953 **Desert Rats.** *Dir:* Robert Wise.

1953 **Stalag 17.** *Dir:* Billy Wilder. *Players:* William Holden, Don Taylor, Otto Preminger, Peter Graves.

1953 **From Here to Eternity.** *Dir:* Fred Zinnemann. *Script:* Daniel Taradash, from James Jones's best-selling novel. *Players:* Burt Lancaster, Montgomery Clift, Deborah Kerr, Frank Sinatra, Ernest Borgnine.

1953 **The Red Beret.** *Dir:* Terence Young.

1953 **The Cruel Sea.** *Dir:* Charles Frend. *Script:* Eric Ambler, from the novel by Nicholas Monsarrat. *Players:* Jack Hawkins, Donald Sinden, John Stratton, Denholm Elliott, Stanley Baker, Liam Redmond, Virginia McKenna.

1953 **Malta Story.** *Dir:* Brian Desmond Hurst. *Players:* Alec Guinness, Jack Hawkins, Anthony Steel, Muriel Pavlow, Flora Robson.

1953 **Albert, R.N.** *Dir:* Lewis Gilbert. *Players:* Anthony Steele, Jack Warner, Robert Beatty, William Sylvester, Anton Diffring, Guy Middleton. Fairly routine P-O-W fare, taken from the stage play by Guy Morgan and Edward Sammis about a dummy created to hide the fact that an escaped prisoner was absent.

1953 **The Last Bridge (Die letzte Brücke).** *Dir:* Helmut Käutner. *Players:* Maria Schell, Bernhard Wicki, Barbara Rütting. Austro-Yugoslavian comment on the futility of war—rather convincing if rather obvious—set among the partisans and their mountains.

1954 **The Colditz Story.** *Dir:* Guy Hamilton. Adapted by the director and producer (Ivan Foxwell) from P. R. Reid's book. *Players:* John Mills, Eric Portman, Christopher Rhodes, Lionel Jeffries, Ian Carmichael, Bryan Forbes.

1954 **The Caine Mutiny.** *Dir:* Edward Dmytryk. *Players:* Humphrey Bogart, Van Johnson, José Ferrer, Fred MacMurray.

1954 **A Generation (Pokolenie).** *Dir:* Andrzej Wajda.

1955 **The Sea Chase.** *Dir:* John Farrow.

1955 **Above Us the Waves.** *Dir:* Ralph Thomas. *Players:* John Mills, John Gregson, Donald Sinden. Very average story of the Battle of the Atlantic, and introducing the German battleship "Tirpitz."

171

Jack Palance, left, appearing to seek instructions as to how to dispose of his German captive: a scene from ATTACK!

A TOWN LIKE ALICE: Peter Finch is unsuccessful in his attempt to rescue Virginia McKenna from grimacing Japs.

1955 **Cockleshell Heroes.** *Dir:* José Ferrer. *Players:* José Ferrer, Trevor Howard, Dora Bryan. Semi-documentary, in the old, old style, about the training of a small group of men to undertake some specific task—in this case attacking blockade-running German ships.

1955 **The Dam Busters.** *Dir:* Michael Anderson. *Players:* Richard Todd, Michael Redgrave, Basil Sydney, Derek Farr, Patrick Barr. The script, taken from books by Paul Brickhill and Guy Gibson (the latter of whom led the raid), was by R. C. Sherriff, of *Journey's End.*

1956 **D-Day: The Sixth of June.** *Dir:* Henry Koster.

1956 **Attack!** *Dir:* Robert Aldrich.

1956 **A Town Like Alice.** *Dir:* Jack Lee. *Players:* Virginia McKenna, Peter Finch. A moderate to fair rendering of Nevil Shute's novel.

1956 **Reach for the Sky.** *Dir:* Lewis Gilbert. *Players:* Kenneth More (as Douglas Bader), Muriel Pavlow, Alexander Knox. The director adapted the script from Paul Brickhill's biography.

1956 **The Battle of the River Plate (The Pursuit of the Graf Spee).** *Dir:* Michael Powell, Emeric Pressburger.

1956 **Kanał.** *Dir:* Andrzej Wajda.

1956 **The Burmese Harp.** *Dir:* Kon Ichikawa.

1956 **The Bold and the Brave.** *Dir:* Lewis R. Foster.

1957 **The Steel Bayonet.** *Dir:* Michael Carreras.

1957 **The Bridge on the River Kwai.** *Dir:* David Lean. *Script:* Pierre Boulle, from his own novel. *Players:* Alec Guinness, Sessue Hayakawa, Jack Hawkins, James Donald, William Holden.

1957 **When Hell Broke Loose.** *Dir:* Kenneth Crane. *Players:* Charles Bronson, Violet Rensing. Incredibility reaches new heights in this tall tale of a no-good-boyo who is forced into the army after Pearl Harbor (as an alternative to prison), and is regenerated as a fighting man through his love for a German girl.

1957 **The Cranes Are Flying (Letyat zhuravli).** *Dir:* Mikhail Kalatozov.

1957 **The Enemy Below.** *Dir:* Dick Powell. *Players:* Robert Mitchum, Curd Jürgens, Theodore Bikel, Russell Collins. A better-than-average submarine drama, strong on suspense, and with notable sound and special effects.

1958 **Ashes and Diamonds (Popioł i diament).** *Dir:* Andrzej Wajda.

1958 **I Was Monty's Double.** *Dir:* John Guillermin. *Players:* John Mills, Cecil Parker, Patrick Allen, Leslie Phillips, Michael Hordern. M. E. Clifton James plays himself—and Montgomery—in this engaging account of his impersonation of the General (as Montgomery then was) in order to bamboozle the Nazis.

1958 **Dunkirk.** *Dir:* Leslie Norman. *Players:* John Mills (seemingly almost permanently engaged in fighting on one front or another during these years), Robert Urquhart, Ray Jackson, Meredith Edwards.

1958 **The Naked and the Dead.** *Dir:* Raoul Walsh. *Players:* Aldo Ray, Cliff Robertson, Raymond Massey. A very watered-down version of Norman Mailer's book—re-made today the result would probably be different, though not necessarily better.

1958 **The Young Lions.** *Dir:* Edward Dmytryk. *Players:* Marlon Brando,

173

The reluctant ambulance: a scene from ICE COLD IN ALEX.

Montgomery Clift, Dean Martin. Irwin Shaw's long and often very effective war novel has been lost somewhere *en route*.

1958 **The Camp on Blood Island.** *Dir:* Val Guest.

1958 **Orders to Kill.** *Dir:* Anthony Asquith. *Script:* Paul Dehn, from a story by D. C. Downes. *Players:* Paul Massie, Eddie Albert, Leslie French, Irene Worth.

1958 **The Battle of the VI.** *Dir:* Vernon Sewell.

1958 **The Silent Enemy.** *Dir:* William Fairchild.

1958 **Ice Cold in Alex.** *Dir:* J. Lee Thompson. *Players:* John Mills, Sylvia Syms, Anthony Quayle, Harry Andrews. Though a straightforward adventure story and little more, this does work up a strong atmosphere of suspense as the commander of a motor ambulance convoy (John Mills) struggles to reach Alexandria in a rickety old vehicle, with assorted companions, after being separated from his unit by the enemy in Libya.

1959 **Ballad of a Soldier (Ballad soldata).** *Dir:* Grigori Chukhray. *Players:* Vladimir Ivashov, Zhanna Prokhorenko.

1959 **The Battle of the Coral Sea.** *Dir:* Paul Wendkos.

1959 **Normandie-Niemen.** *Dir:* Jean Dréville.

1959 **Lotna.** *Dir:* Andrzej Wajda.

1959 **The White Bear (Biały niedzwiedz).** *Dir:* Jerzy Zarzycki.

174

1959   **Battle Inferno.** *Dir:* Frank Wisbar.

1959   **The Bridge (Die Brücke).** *Dir:* Bernhard Wicki. *Players:* Volker Bohnet, Fritz Wepper, Michael Hinz. A much-awarded German anti-war film, set in the final days and concerning the call-up of sixteen-year-old boys to guard an important town bridge.

1959   **Hiroshima mon amour.** *Dir:* Alain Resnais. *Script:* Marguerite Duras. *Players:* Emmanuele Riva, Eiji Okada. *English narrator:* Moira Lister.

1959   **Operation Amsterdam.** *Dir:* Michael McCarthy. *Players:* Peter Finch, Eva Bartok, Tony Britton. A party sets out to German-invaded Holland in May 1940 to rescue the city's store of industrial diamonds. Convincing atmosphere (particularly of the terror of bombardment), reality of setting, brisk pace of action—who would be so churlish as to complain that the characters involved are cardboard?

1959   **Fires on the Plain (Nobi).** *Dir:* Kon Ichikawa.

1960   **Foxhole in Cairo.** *Dir:* John Moxey.

1960   **Blitz on Britain.** A newsreel compilation.

1960   **Sink the Bismarck!** *Dir:* Lewis Gilbert. *Players:* Kenneth More, Dana Wynter, Laurence Naismith. Exciting sea battles with much din and splashing water—and, unfortunately, little else.

1960   **Hell to Eternity.** *Dir:* Phil Karlson.

1960   **The Long and the Short and the Tall.** *Dir:* Leslie Norman. *Script:* Wolf Mankowitz, from the play by Willis Hall. *Players:* Laurence Harvey, Richard Harris, Richard Todd, Ronald Fraser. A reasonably competent filming of the play about a group of soldiers hiding in a jungle hut who capture a Japanese and are unsure what to do with him. A certain suspense, despite much artificiality, both of setting and situation.

1961   **The Guns of Navarone.** *Dir:* J. Lee Thompson. *Players:* Gregory Peck, David Niven, Anthony Quinn, Stanley Baker, Anthony Quayle.

1961   **Tarnished Heroes.** *Dir:* Ernest Morris.

1961   **Reach for Glory.** *Dir:* Philip Leacock. *Script:* John Kohn, Jud Kinberg, John Rae, from the latter's novel, "The Custard Boys." *Players:* Harry Andrews, Kay Walsh, Michael Anderson Jr, Oliver Grimm, Martin Tomlinson, Michael Trubshawe, Cameron Hall, Alan Jeayes.

1961   **The Four Horsemen of the Apocalypse.** *Dir:* Vincente Minnelli. *Players:* Glenn Ford, Ingrid Thulin, Lee J. Cobb, Charles Boyer.

1961   **The Vanishing Corporal (Le caporal épinglé).** *Dir:* Jean Renoir. *Players:* Jean-Pierre Cassel, Claude Brasseur, Claude Rich, O. E. Hasse.

1962   **The Longest Day.** *Dir:* Ken Annakin, Bernhard Wicki, Andrew Marton, Darryl F. Zanuck. *Script:* Cornelius Ryan, from his own book. *Players:* Richard Burton, Kenneth More, Richard Todd, Robert Mitchum, Peter Lawford, Robert Ryan, Henry Fonda, John Wayne, Red Buttons, Jean-Louis Barrault, Arletty, Curd Jürgens, Bourvil, Peter van Eyck.

1962   **The Great Escape.** *Dir:* John Sturges. *Players:* Steve McQueen,

James Garner, Richard Attenborough, James Donald, Charles Bronson, Donald Pleasence.

1962 **Merrill's Marauders.** *Dir:* Samuel Fuller.

1962 **The Four Days of Naples (Le quattro giornate di Napoli).** *Dir:* Nanni Loy.

1962 **The Raiders of Leyte Gulf.** *Dir:* Eddie Romero.

1963 **The Victors.** *Dir:* Carl Foreman. *Script:* Carl Foreman, from "The Human Kind" by A. Baron. *Players:* George Peppard, George Hamilton, Eli Wallach, Vincent Edwards, Mervyn Johns, Melina Mercouri, Romy Schneider, Jeanne Moreau, Senta Berger, Albert Finney.

1963 **Shell Shock.** *Dir:* J. P. Hayes.

1963 **Mystery Submarine.** *Dir:* C. M. Pennington-Richards.

1964 **It Happened Here.** *Dir:* Kevin Brownlow, Andrew Mollo. *Players:* Pauline Murray, Sebastian Shaw, Fiona Leland, Honor Fehrson. *Announcers and commentators:* John Snagge, Alvar Liddell, Frank Phillips, Michael Mellinger.

1964 **The Train.** *Dir:* John Frankenheimer. *Players:* Paul Scofield, Burt Lancaster, Jeanne Moreau, Michel Simon, Suzanne Flon.

1964 **Back Door to Hell.** *Dir:* Monte Hellman.

1964 **633 Squadron.** *Dir:* Walter Grauman. *Players:* Cliff Robertson, George Chakiris, Maria Perschy, Harry Andrews. Once again machines—this time Mosquito planes—prove more watchable than their users, though of its type this is a slightly superior example. Story—project to destroy rocket fuel factory in occupied Norway. Attack successful, after predictable setbacks pending its completion.

1964 **King and Country.** *Dir:* Joseph Losey. *Script:* Evan Jones, from the play "Hamp" by John Wilson, and a story by J. L. Hodson. *Players:* Dirk Bogarde, Tom Courtenay, Leo McKern, Barry Foster, James Villiers, Peter Copley.

1964 **The Secret Invasion.** *Dir:* Roger Corman.

1964 **The Secret of Blood Island.** *Dir:* Quentin Lawrence.

1964 **The Naked Brigade.** *Dir:* Maury Dexter. *Players:* Shirley Eaton, Ken Scott, Mary Chronopolou. A joint USA/Greece venture set in Crete just before the Nazi invasion. Unfortunately a promising idea in a comparatively unexplored theatre of war gets lost in one more tangled triangle.

1965 **In Harm's Way.** *Dir:* Otto Preminger. *Players:* John Wayne, Kirk Douglas, Patricia Neal, Tom Tryon.

1965 **Operation Crossbow.** *Dir:* Michael Anderson. *Players:* George Peppard, Jeremy Kemp, Tom Courtenay, Sophia Loren, Trevor Howard.

1965 **The Battle of the Bulge.** *Dir:* Ken Annakin. *Players:* Henry Fonda, Robert Shaw, Robert Ryan, Dana Andrews, Charles Bronson.

1965 **Is Paris Burning? (Paris brûle-t-il?).** *Dir:* René Clément. *Players:* Orson Welles, Gert Fröbe, Alain Delon, Jean-Pierre Cassel, Jean-Paul Belmondo, Leslie Caron, Glenn Ford, Kirk Douglas, Michel Piccoli, Charles Boyer, Anthony Perkins, Simone Signoret, Yves Montand, Daniel Gélin.

1965 **The Hill.** *Dir:* Sidney Lumet. *Players:* Harry Andrews, Ian Hendry, Sean Connery, Ian Bannen, Michael Redgrave, Alfred Lynch.

Richard Attenborough and Steve McQueen attempt THE GREAT ESCAPE.

Harry Andrews and Sean Connery in Sidney Lumet's unusual and gripping THE HILL.

1965   **King Rat.** *Dir:* Bryan Forbes. *Players:* George Segal, Tom Courtenay,
        James Fox, Denholm Elliott, James Donald, John Mills.
1965   **None but the Brave.** *Dir:* Frank Sinatra. *Players:* Clint Walker,
        Frank Sinatra, Tatsuya Mihashi. Sincerity can sometimes conquer
        cliché, and Sinatra's first film as director, dealing with the growth
        of mutual respect between enemies (Americans and Japanese)
        thrown together in mutual need, is an example of this.
1965   **The Heroes of Telemark.** *Dir:* Anthony Mann. *Players:* Kirk Doug-
        las, Richard Harris, Michael Redgrave, Anton Diffring, Eric Porter,
        Ulla Jacobsson. Visually exciting account of the attempts to sabotage
        Nazi work on discovering the secrets of atomic fission by destroying
        a heavy-water plant in Norway. A pity that the figures are so much
        less interesting than their background.
1965   **Von Ryan's Express.** *Dir:* Mark Robson. *Players:* Frank Sinatra,
        Trevor Howard, Raffaella Carra, Adolfo Celi. Italian trains this
        time—and it is unfortunate they should have come against their
        rivals so closely in Frankenheimer's *The Train.* Nevertheless, as long
        as the train is on screen (which is not long enough) it secures
        attention to itself. And there is always the dependable Trevor
        Howard.
1965   **Up from the Beach.** *Dir:* Robert Parrish.
1965   **Weekend at Dunkirk (Week-end à Zuydcoote).** *Dir:* Henri Verneuil.
        Players: Jean-Paul Belmondo, Catherine Spaak, Georges Géret,
        Kenneth Haigh, Ronald Howard, Nigel Stock. Absolutely chaotic
        dubbing atrocities render this almost impossible to sit through,

Trevor Howard, impressive as always, in VON RYAN'S EXPRESS.

178

The often villainous Marius Goring manhandled by Dirk Bogarde in ILL MET BY MOONLIGHT.

which is a pity because the photography (by Henri Decae) is quite outstanding.

1966 **What Did You Do in the War, Daddy?** *Dir:* Blake Edwards. *Players:* James Coburn, Dick Shawn, Sergio Fantoni, Aldo Ray.

1966 **The Night of the Generals.** *Dir:* Anatole Litvak. *Players:* Peter O'Toole, Omar Sharif, Donald Pleasence, Tom Courtenay, Joanna Pettet, Philippe Noiret. A decided oddity—derived from an "incident" written by James Hadley Chase (of "No Orchids for Miss Blandish"), starting with the murder of a prostitute in 1942 Warsaw and climaxing in the Von Stauffenberg plot of July 1944 to assassinate Hitler.

1966 **Tobruk.** *Dir:* Arthur Hiller.

1967 **The Dirty Dozen.** *Dir:* Robert Aldrich. *Players:* Ernest Borgnine, Lee Marvin, Charles Bronson, John Cassavetes, Robert Ryan, Richard Jaeckel, Telly Savalas.

1967 **The Secret War of Harry Frigg.** *Dir:* Jack Smight. *Players:* Paul Newman, Sylvia Koscina, John Williams, Tom Bosley.

1967 **Beach Red.** *Dir:* Cornel Wilde. *Players:* Cornel Wilde, Burr de Benning, Rip Torn, Patrick Wolfe.

1967 **How I Won the War.** *Dir:* Richard Lester. *Script:* Charles Wood from Patrick Ryan's novel. An anti-war tragi-comic farce-drama that seems to trip over its own feet. In mixing absurd knock-about and grim horror so closely that they become inextricably intertwined, the

179

director has attempted to "show war without kicks." Unfortunately the result is more sick than anything else. The reason for casting Beatle John Lennon is obscure—except of course as regards potential box-office reactions. *Players:* Michael Crawford, John Lennon, Michael Hordern, Roy Kinnear, Jack MacGowran, Lee Montague.

1967 **Attack on the Iron Coast.** *Dir:* Paul Wendkos.

1967 **Submarine X-1.** *Dir:* William Graham.

1967 **Mosquito Squadron.** *Dir:* Boris Sagal.

1967 **Massacre Harbour.** *Dir:* John Peyser.

1968 **The Bridge at Remagen.** *Dir:* John Guillermin. *Players:* George Segal, Robert Vaughn, Ben Gazzara, Bradford Dillman, E. G. Marshall, Peter Van Eyck, Anna Gael.

1968 **The 1,000 Plane Raid.** *Dir:* Boris Sagal. By no means the spectacle that seems to be promised by the title.

1968 **Play Dirty.** *Dir:* André de Toth. *Players:* Michael Caine, Nigel Davenport, Nigel Green, Harry Andrews. A British attempt, apparently to capitalise on the USA/British *The Dirty Dozen*—though why anyone should wish to do so (except in the literal sense) passes comprehension.

1968 **The Long Day's Dying.** *Dir:* Peter Collinson. *Script:* Charles Wood,

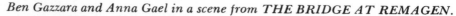

Ben Gazzara and Anna Gael in a scene from THE BRIDGE AT REMAGEN.

'WHAM! The German's rifle is knocked from his hands . . . Sub-Lieut.
Alec Duffy swings into action . . .' So runs the publicity caption to this
scene from ABOVE US THE WAVES. John Gregson is the swinger.

from Alan White's novel. *Players:* David Hemmings, Tom Bell, Tony Beckley, Alan Dobie.

1968 **Where Eagles Dare.** *Dir:* Brian Hutton. *Script:* Alistair MacLean, from his own novel. *Players:* Richard Burton, Clint Eastwood, Patrick Wymark, Michael Hordern, Mary Ure, Peter Barkworth.

1968 **Hannibal Brooks.** *Dir:* Michael Winner. Oliver Reed and Michael J. Pollard escorting an elephant from its bombed-out zoo in Germany to safety in Switzerland. The elephant comes off best.

1968 **A Bullet for Rommel (L'urlo dei giganti).** *Dir:* Henry Mankiewicz.

1968 **Desert Tanks (La battaglia di El Alamein).** *Dir:* Giorgio Ferroni. Italian version of the decisive encounter. As every country attempts to justify its war records, there is presumably no reason why Italy should not do likewise.

1968 **Hell in the Pacific.** *Dir:* John Boorman. *Players:* Lee Marvin, Toshiro Mifune. An American pilot and a Japanese naval officer, neither of whom speaks the other's language, are stranded together on a small atoll in the middle of the Pacific during the closing days of the Second World War. A study of opposing personalities—national and individual—rather than a war story in the narrow sense, and may be regarded as a parable of the difficulties surrounding any attempts to reach true understanding between the essentially different species of the human race.

1968 **The Battle for Anzio.** *Dir:* Edward Dmytryk. *Players:* Robert Mitchum, Peter Falk, Anthony Steele, Patrick Magee, Robert Ryan.

1969 **Battle of Britain.** *Dir:* Guy Hamilton. *Players:* Laurence Olivier, Christopher Plummer, Robert Shaw, Susannah York, Kenneth More, Michael Caine, Ian McShane, Michael Redgrave, Nigel Patrick, Harry Andrews, Trevor Howard, Ralph Richardson.

1969 **The Last Day of the War (El ultimo dia de la guerra).** *Dir:* Juan Antonio Bardem. But not, unfortunately, the last film.

1969 **Patton (G.B.: Patton—Lust for Glory).** *Dir:* Franklin J. Schaffner. *Players:* George C. Scott (as Patton), Karl Malden (as General Omar Bradley), Michael Bates (as Field Marshal Montgomery), Stephen Young, Michael Strong, Karl Michael Vogler (as Rommel), Gerald Flood, Peter Barkworth, Tim Considine (as the slapped soldier).

1969 **The Last Escape.** *Dir:* Walter Grauman.

1969 **Too Late the Hero.** *Dir:* Robert Aldrich. *Players:* Michael Caine, Cliff Robertson, Ian Bannen, Harry Andrews, Ronald Fraser.

1969 **The Great Battle (Osvobozhdyeniye).** *Dir:* Yuri Ozerov. *Players:* Buhuti Zakariadze (as Stalin), Yuri Durov (as Churchill), Fritz Ditz (as Hitler).

1970 **Catch-22.** *Dir:* Mike Nichols. *Script:* Buck Henry, from Joseph Heller's novel. *Players:* Alan Arkin, Martin Balsam, Richard Benjamin, Art Garfunkel, Anthony Perkins, Jon Voight, Orson Welles.

1970 **Kelly's Heroes.** *Dir:* Brian G. Hutton.

1970 **Tora! Tora! Tora!** *Dir:* Richard Fleischer. *Players:* Joseph Cotten, Martin Balsam, E. G. Marshall, James Whitmore, Jason Robards, Tatsuya Mihashi, Takahiro Tamura. The Japanese sequences were

182

directed by Toshio Masuda and Kinji Fukasaku.

1970 **Ja, Ja, Mein General! But Which Way to the Front?** *Dir:* Jerry Lewis. A typically over-strained Jerry Lewis performance, but with some undeniably amusing gags.

1971 **Murphy's War.** *Dir:* Peter Yates. *Players:* Peter O'Toole, Sian Phillips, Philippe Noiret, Horst Janson.

Peter O'Toole in MURPHY'S WAR.

The Korean War (1950-53)

1951 Why Korea? Newsreel apologia.

1951 **Korea Patrol.** *Dir:* Max Nosseck. One of the first of a dismally similar procession.

1951 **Steel Helmet.** *Dir:* Samuel Fuller.

1951 **Fixed Bayonets.** *Dir:* Samuel Fuller.

1952 **Battle Zone.** *Dir:* Lesley Selander.

1952 **One Minute to Zero.** *Dir:* Tay Garnett.

1952 **Retreat, Hell!** *Dir:* Joseph Lewis.

1953 **Cease Fire.** *Dir:* Owen Crump.

1953 **The Glory Brigade.** *Dir:* Robert D. Webb. *Players:* Victor Mature, Lee Marvin, Richard Egan, Alexander Scourby. Slightly more intelligent than the general run, and dealing with the possibility that even allies might not have unlimited confidence in, or feel excessive friendship for, one another.

1954 **Prisoner of War.** *Dir:* Andrew Marton.

1954 **The Bridges at Toko-Ri.** *Dir:* Mark Robson. *Players:* William Holden, Grace Kelly, Fredric March, Mickey Rooney. The distinguished cast ensures interesting performances and the script (from a novel by James A. Michener) is more literate and pointed than the general rut. Story, behind and before scenes of a bombing raid, much as usual.

1954 **Take the High Ground.** *Dir:* Richard Brooks. *Players:* Richard Widmark, Karl Malden, Carleton Carpenter. Training and introduction to combat of a group of conscriped men. Familiar ground, covered incomparably better by Carol Reed during the Second World War.

1954 **Dragonfly Squadron.** *Dir:* Lesley Selander.

1954 **Prisoner of War.** *Dir:* Andrew Marton.

1956 **Battle Hymn.** *Dir:* Douglas Sirk. *Players:* Rock Hudson, Anna Kashfi, Dan Duryea, Don DeFore. Another of those terrible affairs (based, it seems, on truth) about the fighting preacher who manages to face in all directions at once.

1957 **Men in War.** *Dir:* Anthony Mann. *Players:* Robert Ryan, Aldo Ray, Robert Keith, Philip Pine, Vic Morrow, Nehemiah Persoff.

1960 **War Hero.** *Dir:* Burt Topper.

1961 **Marines, Let's Go.** *Dir:* Raoul Walsh.

1961 **War Hunt.** *Dir:* Denis Sanders.

1962 **Hell Is for Heroes.** *Dir:* Don Siegel.

1962 **The Nun and the Sergeant.** *Dir:* Franklin Adreon. As dire as the expectations aroused by its title.

1969 **M*A*S*H.** *Dir:* Robert Altman. *Script:* Ring Lardner Jr, from a novel by Richard Hooker. *Players:* Donald Sutherland, Elliott Gould, Tom Skerritt, Sally Kellerman, Robert Duvall, Jo Ann Pflug, Rene Auberjonois, David Arkin, Roger Bowen, Bud Cort.

Vietnam

1965   **Commandos in Vietnam.** *Dir:* Marshall Thompson. Propaganda; simple, if less than pure.

1965   **Pierrot le fou.** *Dir:* Jean-Luc Godard. The film contains a sequence featuring the Vietnamese war in terms of a pantomimic burlesque.

1967   **Far from Vietnam (Loin du Viêt-Nam).** *Dir:* Alain Resnais, William Klein, Joris Ivens, Agnès Varda, Claude Lelouch, Jean-Luc Godard.

1968   **The Green Berets.** *Dir:* John Wayne, Ray Kellogg. *Players:* John Wayne, David Janssen, Jim Hutton, Aldo Ray, Raymond St Jacques, Bruce Cabot, Patrick Wayne, Luke Askew, Jack Soo, George Takei.

The Atomic Threat (1945-?)

1950   **Seven Days to Noon.** *Dir:* John Boulting. *Script:* Frank Harvey, Roy Boulting, from a story by Paul Dehn and James Bernard. *Players:* Barry Jones, Olive Sloane, André Morell, Joan Hickson.

John Wayne, who co-directed as well as starring, at work with the cameras on THE GREEN BERETS.

1959   **On the Beach.** *Dir:* Stanley Kramer. *Players:* Gregory Peck, Fred Astaire, Anthony Perkins, Ava Gardner.

1964   **Dr Strangelove, or How I Learned to Stop Worrying and Love the Bomb.** *Dir:* Stanley Kubrick. *Script:* Stanley Kubrick, Terry Southern, Peter George, from the latter's novel, "Red Alert." *Players:* Peter Sellers, Sterling Hayden, George C. Scott, Slim Pickens, Keenan Wynn, Peter Bull.

1964   **Fail-Safe.** *Dir:* Sidney Lumet. *Players:* Henry Fonda, Dan O'Herlihy, Walter Matthau, Frank Overton, Russell Hardie, Russell Collins.

1965   **The Bedford Incident.** *Dir:* James B. Harris. *Players:* Richard Widmark, Eric Portman, Martin Balsam, James MacArthur, Sidney Poitier.

1965   **The War Game.** *Dir:* Peter Watkins, from his own script. *Narrators:* Michael Aspel, Dick Graham.

Index

NOTE: Where comments, in addition to those in the text, are made on films in the Chronological List, the relevant page number is entered in the Index.